ADAPTATION AND APPROPRIATION

From the apparently simple *adaptation* of a text into film, theatre or a new literary work, to the more complex *appropriation* of style or meaning, it is arguable that all texts are somehow connected to a network of existing texts and art forms.

Adaptation and Appropriation explores:

- multiple definitions and practices of adaptation and appropriation
- the cultural and aesthetic politics behind the impulse to adapt
- diverse ways in which contemporary literature and film adapt, revise and reimagine other works of art
- the impact on adaptation and appropriation of theoretical movements, including structuralism, post-structuralism, postcolonialism, postmodernism, feminism and gender studies
- the appropriation across time and across cultures of specific canonical texts, but also of literary archetypes such as myth or fairy tale

Ranging across genres and harnessing concepts from fields as diverse as musicology and the natural sciences, this volume brings clarity to the complex debates around adaptation and appropriation, offering a much-needed resource for those studying literature, film or culture.

Julie Sanders is Professor of English Literature and Drama at the University of Nottingham.

THE NEW CRITICAL IDIOM

SERIES EDITOR: JOHN DRAKAKIS, UNIVERSITY OF STIRLING

The New Critical Idiom is an invaluable series of introductory guides to today's critical terminology. Each book:

- provides a handy, explanatory guide to the use (and abuse) of the term
- offers an original and distinctive overview by a leading literary and cultural critic
- relates the term to the larger field of cultural representation

With a strong emphasis on clarity, lively debate and the widest possible breadth of examples, *The New Critical Idiom* is an indispensable approach to key topics in literary studies.

Also available in this series:

ADAPTATION AND APPROPRIATION

Julie Sanders

Routledge
Taylor & Francis Group

LONDON AND NEW YORK

First published 2006 by Routledge
2 Park Square, Milton Park, Abingdon, Oxon OX14 4RN

Simultaneously published in the USA and Canada
by Routledge
270 Madison Ave, New York, 10016

Reprinted 2007, 2008, 2010

*Routledge is an imprint of the Taylor & Francis Group,
an informa business*

Typeset in Garamond and ScalaSans by Taylor & Francis Books
Printed and bound in Great Britain
by TJ International Ltd, Padstow, Cornwall

British Library Cataloguing in Publication Data
A catalogue record for this book is available from the British Library

Library of Congress Cataloging in Publication Data
Sanders, Julie.
 Adaptation and appropriation / Julie Sanders.
   p. cm. -- (The new critical idiom)
 Includes bibliographical references and index.
 ISBN 0-415-31171-3 (hardback : alk. paper) -- ISBN 0-415-31172-1
(pbk. : alk. paper) 1. Literature--Adaptations. I. Title. II. Series.
 PN171.A33S26 2005
 801--dc22

                              2005008610

ISBN10: 0–415–31171–3 (hbk)   ISBN13: 978–0–415–31171–7(hbk)
ISBN10: 0–415–31172–1 (pbk)   ISBN13: 978–0–415–31172–4(pbk)

Taylor & Francis Group is the Academic Division of T&F Informa plc.

For Gaynor Macfarlane

One who really loves texts must wish from time to time to love (at least) two together

Gérard Genette, *Palimpsests*

There were, as in all crooked businesses, two sets of books ...

Peter Carey, *Jack Maggs*

CONTENTS

SERIES EDITOR'S PREFACE

The New Critical Idiom is a series of introductory books which seeks to extend the lexicon of literary terms, in order to address the radical changes which have taken place in the study of literature during the last decades of the twentieth century. The aim is to provide clear, well-illustrated accounts of the full range of terminology currently in use, and to evolve histories of its changing usage.

The current state of the discipline of literary studies is one where there is considerable debate concerning basic questions of terminology. This involves, among other things, the boundaries which distinguish the literary from the non-literary; the position of literature within the larger sphere of culture; the relationship between literatures of different cultures; and questions concerning the relation of literary to other cultural forms within the context of interdisciplinary studies.

It is clear that the field of literary criticism and theory is a dynamic and heterogeneous one. The present need is for individual volumes on terms which combine clarity of exposition with an adventurousness of perspective and a breadth of application. Each volume will contain as part of its apparatus some indication of the direction in which the definition of particular terms is likely to move, as well as expanding the disciplinary boundaries within which some of these terms have been traditionally contained. This will involve some re-situation of terms within the larger field of cultural representation, and will introduce examples from the area of film and the modern media in addition to examples from a variety of literary texts.

ACKNOWLEDGEMENTS

As this volume evidences, few stories or books ever stand alone and with that in mind I would like to acknowledge those who have contributed to this book. Fred Botting read and commented on the original proposal with great insight and made the final outline much stronger. Many others have offered ideas and help along the way; special thanks to Kate Chedgzoy, Davina Cooper, Mark Dooley, Finn Fordham, Daniel Grimley, Dominic Head, Barbara Kelly, Máire ní Fhlathúin, Mark Robson, Kiernan Ryan, Michael Sanders, Lauren Shohet and Tory Young, as well as all the students at Keele and Nottingham who have offered their various perspectives and enthusiasms on this topic. The University of Teesside provided a valuable audience for some of this work in its early stages and I am grateful to all who attended and contributed on that occasion. I underwent my own process of professional adaptation while writing this volume and I thank my new colleagues at the University of Nottingham for making me feel so very welcome. Though they will probably never know it, the Quadriga Consort and the virtuoso musicianship of Andrew Manze were my joint inspiration for the baroque musical theories deployed in these pages and I am endlessly indebted both to the intellect of their sleeve-notes and the beauty of their playing. Richard Powers's remarkable novel, first gifted me by my father, *The Gold Bug Variations*, and Glenn Gould's remarkable 1955 and 1981 interpretations of Bach's *Goldberg Variations* provided the literary and musical soundtrack to much of the thinking laid out here.

My series editor John Drakakis has been a model of sound advice, good readership, and great wit, and Liz Thompson at Routledge shaped the volume in several crucial ways; I only hope the final book does them both justice. John Higham has been my other, and better, half throughout the enterprise; during that time he has performed for real the acts of grafting that I can only invoke as metaphor, bringing things to fruition with a very tangible beauty, and, as ever, I thank him.

The book is dedicated to Gaynor, my best pal, with love and thanks for sharing the journey over many years.

INTRODUCTION

art never improves, but ... the material of art is never quite the same.
T. S. Eliot, 'Tradition and the Individual Talent'

This book is concerned with the literariness of literature. Any exploration of intertextuality, and its specific manifestation in the forms of
adaptation and appropriation, is inevitably interested in how art creates
art, or how literature is made by literature. There is a danger, however,
that this activity of investigating or 'reading' adaptations proves rather
self-serving, merely stimulating the afterlife of texts and therefore of literary criticism as a scholarly pursuit. The literary academic or student
reads many texts throughout their learning career and the more texts
they read the more echoes, parallels, and points of comparison they
identify in the texts that they encounter. The notion that the tracing of
intertextual reference and allusion is a self-confirming exercise is reasonable enough – Robert Weimann writes persuasively of the 'reproductive
dimension of appropriation' (1983: 14), suggesting the manifold ways
in which texts feed off and create other texts – but, as readers and critics, we also need to recognize that adaptation and appropriation are fundamental to the practice, and, indeed, to the enjoyment, of literature.

The late twentieth century made a particular virtue out of querying
the ability or even necessity of being 'original', not least in the arts.
Edward Said suggested in 'On Originality' that 'the writer thinks less of

writing originally, and more of rewriting' (1983: 135); Jacques Derrida noted that 'the desire to write is the desire to launch things that come back to you as much as possible' (1985: 157). The 'rewriting' impulse, which is much more than simple imitation, is often articulated in theoretical terms such as intertextuality, and many prominent theorists of this practice emerge from the structuralist and poststructuralist movements of the 1960s, especially in France. In the field of anthropology, Claude Lévi-Strauss conducted many of his researches in terms of identifying repeating structures across cultures (2001 [1978]). In the literary sphere, Roland Barthes declared that 'any text is an intertext' (1981: 39), suggesting that the works of previous and surrounding cultures were always present in literature. Barthes also highlighted the ways in which texts were not solely dependent on their authors for the production of meaning, indicating how they benefited from readers who created their own intertextual networks. Julia Kristeva, herself a product of scientific and anthropological training under Lévi-Strauss, formulated the term *intertextualité* in her essay 'The Bounded Text' to describe the process by which any text was 'a permutation of texts, an intertextuality' (1980: 36). Kristeva's focus was driven by semiotics; she was interested in how texts were permeated by the signs, signifiers, and utterances of the culture in which they participated, or from which they derived. Intertextuality as a term has, however, come to refer to a far more textual as opposed to utterance-driven notion of how texts encompass and respond to other texts both during the process of their creation and composition and in terms of the individual reader's or spectator's response.

Adaptations and appropriations can vary in how explicitly they state their intertextual purpose. Many of the film, television, or theatre adaptations of canonical works of literature that we look at in this volume openly declare themselves as an interpretation or re-reading of a canonical precursor. Sometimes this will involve a director's personal vision, and it may or may not involve cultural relocation or updating of some form; sometimes this reinterpretative act will also involve the movement into a new generic mode or context. In appropriations the intertextual relationship may be less explicit, more embedded, but what is often inescapable is the fact that a political or ethical commitment shapes a writer's, director's, or performer's decision to re-interpret a source text. In this respect, in any study of adaptation and appropriation the creative import of the author cannot be as easily dismissed as Roland Barthes's or Michel Foucault's influential theories of the 'death of the author' might suggest (Barthes 1988; Foucault 1979). Nevertheless the ability of these theories to destabilize the authority of the original text does enable multiple and sometimes conflicting production of meaning, a fact that will prove important for our analyses. The inherent intertextuality of literature encourages the ongoing, evolving production of meaning, and an ever-expanding network of textual relations.

Literary texts 'are built from systems, codes and traditions established by previous works of literature' (Allen 2000: 1). But they are also built from systems, codes, and traditions derived from companion art forms. If Kristeva is credited with formulating the theory of intertextuality, hers was a theory that was far from exclusive in its application to literature. She saw art, music, drama, dance, and literature in terms of a living mosaic, a dynamic intersection of textual surfaces. We might wish to add film to this list, but following the Kristevan model, much of the terminology adopted by this study to describe literary adaptation and appropriation is harnessed from the parallel disciplines of fine art and musicology. The vocabulary of adaptation is highly labile: Adrian Poole has offered an extensive list of terms to represent the Victorian era's interest in reworking the artistic past: '(in no particular order) ... borrowing, stealing, appropriating, inheriting, assimilating ... being influenced, inspired, dependent, indebted, haunted, possessed ... homage, mimicry, travesty, echo, allusion, and intertextuality' (2004: 2). We could continue the linguistic riff, adding into the mix: variation, version, interpretation, imitation, proximation, supplement, increment, improvisation, prequel, sequel, continuation, addition, paratext, hypertext, palimpsest, graft, rewriting, reworking, refashioning, re-vision, re-evaluation. The glossary at the back of this volume grapples with a small selection of these terms but embedded within the pages of the book the reader will encounter many more. I make no apologies for the profusion rather than fixity of terms offered: the idiom in which adaptation and appropriation functions is rich and various; that is part of its essence and importance, and any study of the same should surely reflect this fact.

J. Hillis Miller has explored various permutations of the paratextual, the peritextual, and the hypertextual in his critical writings, delineating the multifarious ways in which a literary text can be 'inhabited ... by a long chain of parasitical presences, echoes, allusions, guests, ghosts of previous texts' (Gilbert and Gubar 2000 [1979]: 46). This volume concerns itself at various turns with these textual ghosts and hauntings, both literal and metaphorical. In turn, questions of dependency and derivation are broached. Studies of adaptation and appropriation invariably conjure up questions of ownership and the attendant legal discourses of copyright and property law. Following on from Barthes's destabilization of fixed textual meaning, however, as both procedure and process, adaptation and appropriation are celebratory of the cooperative and collaborative model.

Certain distinctions remain, nevertheless, crucial to understanding the operations of adaptation and appropriation. There is a need, for example, to distinguish between direct quotation and acts of citation. Quotation can be deferential or critical, supportive or questioning; it depends on the context in which the quotation takes place. Citation, however, presumes a more deferential relationship; it is frequently self-authenticating, even reverential, in its reference to the canon of 'authoritative', culturally validated, texts. Many nineteenth-century novels, those of Thomas Hardy, the Brontë sisters, and George Eliot, for example, deployed Shakespearean citation in this manner. But citation is different again to adaptation, which constitutes a more sustained engagement with a single text or source than the more glancing act of allusion or quotation, even citation, allows. Beyond that, appropriation carries out the same sustained engagement as adaptation but frequently adopts a posture of critique, even assault.

Adaptation and appropriation are inevitably involved in the performance of textual echo and allusion, but this does not usually equate to the fragmentary *bricolage* of quotation more commonly understood as the operative mode of intertextuality. In French, *bricolage* is the term for 'Do-it-yourself' (DIY), which helps to explain its application in a literary context to those texts that assemble a range of quotations, allusions, and citations from existent works of art. A parallel form in art is the creation of *collage* by assembling found items to create a new aesthetic object or in music the creative act of 'sampling'. This purposeful reassembly of fragments to form a new whole is, undoubtedly, an active element in many of the postmodernist texts explored in the course of this study.

There are also important ways in which the act of *bricolage* shades into the literary practice of pastiche. Pastiche is another term of French derivation which in the musical sphere refers to a medley of references, a composition made up of fragments pieced together (Dentith, 2000: 194). In the domains of art and literature, however, pastiche has undergone a further shift or extension of reference, being applied most often to those works which carry out an extended imitation of the style of a single artist or writer. There are, undoubtedly, some current novelists who are exponents of the medley style of pastiche – Jonathan Coe, for example, in his richly allusive *What a Carve Up!* (1994), which mimics everything from journalism to James Joyce in the course of its narrative – but frequently it is the more sustained act of artistic imitation which is accorded the label of pastiche in contemporary literature. Pastiche is often assumed to have a satiric undertow or a parodic intention, although there are exceptions to this rule. In some respects there is often a complicated blend of admiration and satire at play in pastiches of particular authors or literary styles. J. M. Coetzee's *Foe*, discussed in detail in Chapter 6, reworks with both celebratory and satiric intent the aesthetics of eighteenth-century prose, and the writings of Daniel Defoe in particular, in its version of novels written in the epistolary or journalistic style; Peter Carey effects something similar in his self-conscious revisiting of the tropes and idioms of nineteenth-century fiction, and in particular Dickensian narrative, in *Jack Maggs*, explored in Chapter 7. There are also, in both these novels, moments when *bricolage* and pastiche are jointly in play, but, on the whole, when assigning a political or ethical commitment to acts of literary appropriation such as these postcolonial rewritings of canonical texts (*Robinson Crusoe* and *Great Expectations* respectively), we acknowledge that stylistic imitation is neither the essence nor sole purpose of the approach to the source text, even though it may be a defining feature.

James Joyce's 1922 novel *Ulysses* could be viewed as the archetype of the adaptive text. The title alone indicates a structuring relationship with Homer's Ancient Greek epic of the wandering and journeying Ulysses (also known as Odysseus): *The Odyssey*. That relationship was even more apparent in the pre-publication instalments of Joyce's novel where each chapter heading signified a specific relationship with an event or character in the Homeric narrative: 'Telemachus'; 'Lotus

Eaters'; 'Scylla and Charybdis'; 'Sirens'; 'Circe'; 'Penelope'. Joyce's decision to suppress these referential chapter headings in the final published version of the novel raises the question as to whether we require knowledge of *The Odyssey* to understand in any comprehensive sense his Dublin narrative. What this question highlights, however, is the fundamental contradictory impulse towards dependence and liberation implicit in the majority of the adaptations and appropriations that will be invoked in the course of this volume. Gérard Genette has categorized *Ulysses* as 'the very type of the self-proclaimed hypertext' and yet as 'an extreme case of emancipation from the hypotext' (1997: 309), with 'hypertext' here equating to the adaptation and 'hypotext' to the source. Joyce's novel can undoubtedly be read alone and appreciated as a narrative, as a remarkable vignette of a day in the life of an ensemble of Dublin inhabitants in the 1920s; this is by no means a failed or insufficient reading. And yet a reading of that narrative alongside an informing awareness of the events of Homer's epic clearly enriches the potential for the production of meaning, so that we see, as Jennifer Levine has noted, the quasi-father–son relationship that emerges between Stephen Daedalus and Leopold Bloom in the novel as suggestive in its own right and yet register how 'it sharpens our sense of the potentially filial relationship between them to see them also as Telemachus and Odysseus' (1990: 32). Of course, the intertextuality of Joyce's characters does not rest with the Homeric comparisons alone, since Stephen and Leopold's relationship also suggests that of Hamlet and Old Hamlet, and *Ulysses* resonates with Shakespearean echoes and refrains. Elsewhere the narrative indulges in numerous virtuoso performances of literary pastiche.

If Leopold's wife, Molly, who speaks the infamous closing monologue of *Ulysses*, is a version of Odysseus's wife, Penelope, patiently awaiting her wandering husband's return from his epic adventures, there is also a self-conscious rewriting of the informing sourcetext in the fact that Molly proves a distinctly adulterous version of the archetypal loyal wife. Joyce expands the frame of reference further by evoking Shakespeare's wife, Ann Hathaway, as another Penelope, since she was left behind in Stratford-upon-Avon when the playwright went to London to make his name: 'We begin to be interested in Mrs S' (Joyce 1986 [1922]: 165). There is often humour as well as intellectual richness at work in the parallels and consonances Joyce evokes. This Irish epic compresses the decades and continents of the Homeric text into a single Dublin day, punctuated by pub gatherings, and cooking on the stove. Cyclops becomes an obstructive drinker in Barney Kiernan's bar, Circe a brothel owner. There is undoubtedly an element of parody, or the 'mock-epic', implicit in this approach, comparable to Alexander Pope's reduction of the epic form to a story of a vain woman at her dressing table in his long eighteenth-century poem 'The Rape of the Lock'. In this respect, *Ulysses* embodies the reduction and compression that Genette has identified as a common impulse in some hypertextual literature and yet in its verbal complexity and twisting, web-like narrative *Ulysses* also deserves recognition for its art of amplification: making the quotidian lives of its Dublin community epic in scope. An intertextual reading of *Ulysses* draws readers' imaginations into the realms of Homer, Dante and Shakespeare, stretching far beyond its self-proclaimed horizons and cultural geography. The signifying field appears vast as a result.

Ulysses is a potent reminder of the rich possibilities of the adaptive technique and of readings alert to the politics of appropriation, but it is also a fine example of the sense of play that many theorists have stressed as central to the adaptive instinct. Paul Ricoeur describes appropriation as 'the "playful" transposition of the text, and play itself ... as the modality appropriate to the reader *potentialis*, that is, to anyone who can read' (1991: 87). As this volume will stress, there is frequently heartfelt political commitment standing behind acts of literary appropriation or 're-vision'. Adrienne Rich's coining of this phrase with its crucial inserted hyphen was a product of her personal feminist and lesbian politics (1992 [1971]). But the political aspect of 're-visionary' writing should never occlude the simultaneously pleasurable aspects of reading into such texts their intertextual and allusive relationship with other texts, tracing and activating the networks of association that we have been describing. As Genette observes: 'one who really loves texts must wish from time to time to love (at least) two together' (1997 [1982]: 399). Such statements encourage us to categorize and define adaptation and appropriation and their cultural histories while at the same time taking care to ensure that these elements of pleasure are neither lost nor underestimated.

T. S. Eliot's 1919 essay 'Tradition and the Individual Talent' has been described as 'perhaps the single most formative work in twentieth-century Anglo-American criticism' (Widdowson 1999: 49). Eliot's essay is certainly essential reading for students of adaptation and appropriation. Eliot sought to rethink notions of originality and value, querying the 'tendency to insist, when we praise a poet, upon those aspects of his work in which he least resembles anyone else' (Eliot 1984 [1919]: 37). The unapologetically masculinist emphasis aside, Eliot's comments are pertinent to this project. Suggesting an alternative literary value-system in which the reworking and response to the texts of the past would take centre-stage, Eliot questioned why originality was valued over 'repetition': 'No poet, no artist, of any art, has his complete meaning alone' (38). He was not advocating blind adherence to precursor texts or ages, an action that would after all be little more than literary plagiarism; his notion of the 'individual talent' was that it created new material upon the surface and foundation of the literary past.

Peter Widdowson is correct to acknowledge that Eliot's case for an historical awareness of literary tradition served to justify his own intertextual, discursive style and the aims of the Modernist movement (1999: 49). Modernist poetry, not least Eliot's own, practised intertextuality in the form of quotation, allusion, collage, *bricolage*, and fragment. As already stressed, in this study we are looking at something rather different, a more sustained engagement between texts and their creators. We are seeking to theorize an interrelation between texts which is fundamental to their existence and which at times seems to get to the heart of the literary, and especially the reading, experience. Eliot's delineation of the 'historical sense' (1984 [1919]: 38) is helpful; he suggests that meaning stems from the relationships between texts, relationships which encourage contrast and comparison. As the close readings conducted here underline, this is exactly what an aesthetic and historicized critical study of adaptation is concerned with.

Eliot's essay has sometimes been attacked on the grounds that it implicitly assumes a literary canon, a series of valued texts that are (re)turned to and consulted by subsequent ages (Eagleton 1994 [1981]: 54). The debate that has raged around canon formation in literary studies in recent decades is inescapable in this context. Adaptation both appears to require and to perpetuate the existence of a canon, although it may in turn contribute to its ongoing reformulation and expansion. As Derek Attridge has astutely observed: 'The perpetuation of any canon is dependent in part on the references made to its earlier members by its later members (or would-be members) ...' (1996: 169). The required 'reading alongside' of source and adaptation, the signifiers respectively of 'tradition' and 'individual talent' in Eliot's terminology, demands a knowledge on the part of the reader (or spectator) of the source when encountering the derivative or responsive text. In this respect, adaptation becomes a veritable marker of canonical status; citation infers authority.

To this end, adaptation could be defined as an inherently conservative genre. As Attridge continues: 'through their frequently overt *allusiveness* ... novels offer themselves not as challenges to the canon, but as canonic – as already canonized, one might say. They appear to locate themselves within an established literary culture, rather than presenting themselves as an assault on that culture' (1996: 169). Yet, as the notion of hostile takeover present in a term such as 'appropriation' implies, adaptation can also be oppositional, even subversive. There are as many opportunities for divergence as adherence, for assault as well as homage.

Another influential essay for studies of appropriation, then, is Adrienne Rich's 'When We Dead Awaken: Writing as Re-vision', first published in 1971. In that essay she made the much-cited observation that for women writers it was essential to take on the writing of the past in order to move beyond it into a free (liberated) creative space of their own: 'Re-vision – the act of looking back, of seeing with fresh eyes, of entering an old text from a new critical direction ... We need to know the writing of the past and know it differently than we have ever known it; not to pass on a tradition but to break its hold over us' (Rich 1992 [1971]: 369). The suggestion is similar to Eliot's in that it invokes the literary past and insists on an historical understanding to foster creativity both in the present and in the future, but it is also entirely antithetical to Eliot's mindset in that it simultaneously advocates a radical break with that tradition, a dissonant and dissident rupturing of its value-systems and hierarchies. This critical perspective on the relationship between tradition and the individual talent is one shared by writers producing work from feminist, gay and lesbian, and postcolonial subject-positions.

Another theorist of literature's relationship to its own past whose work is both acknowledged and challenged by these subject-positions is Harold Bloom. His seminal book *The Anxiety of Influence*, first published in 1973, considered the fraught relationship between writers and their literary inheritance, constructing it in self-consciously Freudian terms as an Oedipal struggle between young 'sons' and their literary forefathers. Several flaws in this argument have subsequently been exposed, not least that Bloom writes from an exclusively masculinist position. He also constructs a very particular literary history, one with an emphasis on the individual creator or literary 'genius', and therefore one that unduly privileges the Romantic era when a special stress on the individual creative mind and the unique personal contribution of the poet emerged. Several critics have since traced alternative teleologies of literary influence, indicating, for example, the impact of the classics on early modern writers such as Shakespeare (Bate 1993), and acknowledging a strong female presence within the communities of influence as well as those influenced (Gilbert and Gubar 2000 [1979]). Nevertheless, Bloom's central thesis of 'misprision', the often happenstance or inevitable reinterpretation of texts during the process of adoption, translation, and reworking them into new contexts, remains a highly suggestive one for appropriation studies and one which has influenced the vocabulary with which many scholars operate in this field.

The central problem with any tradition is the ability to recognize not only those who constitute that tradition but those who are at various times excluded from it, or, at the very least, consigned to its margins. Henry Louis Gates Jr has examined this phenomenon in relation to African-American writing, a literary domain that in its desire to assert its own methodologies and ways of operating, nevertheless found a need to confront the white literary tradition within its pages; this is what Graham Allen has described as the 'struggle of black subjects to enter into Western literary culture' (2000: 168). For Allen, 'The core of Gates's argument is that African-American writing is double-voiced and self-consciously intertextual in its relation to both standard English and a black vernacular discourse ...' (2000: 168). Gates's most expansive discussion of these ideas takes place in *The Signifying Monkey* (1988), and invokes the crucial analogue of jazz music and the improvisational yet allusive techniques it deploys: 'In the jazz tradition, compositions by Count Basie ("signify") and Oscar Peterson ("signifyin'") are structured around the idea of formal revision and implication' (Gates 1988: 123). This discussion of adaptation and appropriation will invoke the example of jazz on several occasions, and of musicology on several more. But the specific relevance to African-American writing of 'signifying' and its relationship to jazz deserves notice. As James Andreas Sr acknowledges: 'To signify in African and African-American cultures is to improvise upon a given *topos*, narrative, or joke the way a jazz musician improvises on a progression of chords, melodic structure, or spontaneous riff in the previous musician's solo' (1999: 107). Andreas Sr's specific example of this in action is the work of Gloria Naylor. Her novels have been much studied due to their intertextuality with Shakespeare, Faulkner, Dante, Chaucer, and the Bible among others (Erickson 1996). In *Bailey's Cafe*, this signifying practice is played out through a complex series of layers, allusions, and shaping influences. The café of the title is a literal space in the novel but one that appears able to cross geographical and temporal borders. The characters who visit the café each have a tale to tell and their tales are reworkings of biblical ones, including those of Eve and Mariam. The intertextuality does not stop there, for the name of the café as well as the characters' tale-telling invokes a seminal work of English medieval literature: in Chaucer's *The Canterbury Tales*, the host of the Tabard Inn where the pilgrims gathered before their journey to Canterbury, and who proposed that they tell their individual stories en route, was called Harry Bailey.

Shakespeare, a familiar hypotext throughout Naylor's *oeuvre*, is present in the novel's evocations of *The Tempest* among other texts (Sanders 2001: 170–90), but it is the manner in which the narrative structure is shaped by movements more familiar from the musical domains of blues and jazz that seems most overtly to acknowledge Gates's theories. Sections entitled 'Mood Indigo' and 'Miss Maple's Blues' explicitly acknowledge the literary riffs and improvisations being effected by Naylor on a diverse range of influences and sources. Naylor is a writer steeped in other writers and yet her voice remains distinctly her own; Gates suggests this is a typical feature of African-American writing, which consciously positions itself in relation to canonical (white) Western culture and the companion productions of fellow African and African-American writers. As Andreas Sr notes in his discussion of Naylor's *Tempest*-soaked appropriation *Mama Day*, her work embodies the familiar African-American practice of 'playful but wilful manipulation of the signifier [that] alters perception of the signified ...' (1999: 107).

In all of the instances discussed in this introduction, and elsewhere in this volume, the 'rewrite', be it in the form of novel, play, poem or film, invariably transcends mere imitation, serving instead in the capacity of incremental literature (Zabus 2002: 4), adding, supplementing, improvising, innovating. The aim is not replication as such, but rather complication, expansion rather than contraction (Andreas 1999: 107). In scientific terms, we might speak about the crucial difference between a clone and a genetic adaptation. And if musicology offers us one highly applicable and suggestive set of metaphors and idioms for conducting a discussion of literary adaptation and appropriation within these pages, it will also be registered that the scientific domain of genetics, stretching from the nineteenth-century horticultural experiments of Gregor Mendel and Charles Darwin's controversial theory of natural selection and environmental adaptation through to the research into DNA in the twentieth century, provides a further set of productive correspondences.

Using a separate field of terminology derived from the world of horticulture, Genette has written at length about the 'palimpsestuous nature of texts', observing that 'Any text is a hypertext, grafting itself onto a hypotext, an earlier text that it imitates or transforms' (1997 [1982]: ix). Grafting is just one of several creative metaphors for the adaptive process that this volume will favour. As Chapter 2 explores further, there is a need to establish a more diverse vocabulary for discussing and describing the relationship between texts and hypertext, source and appropriation, than these labels at present enable. In these phrases the relationship is often viewed as linear and reductive; the appropriation is always in the secondary, belated position, and the discussion will therefore always be, to a certain extent, about difference, lack, or loss. Travel can change for the better though, so the metaphor of the journey may still be helpful, even though it implies a linear movement from point A to point B.

By eschewing a linear epistemology altogether, however, phrases such as 'grafting' or models derived from musicology, which allow for greater dynamic impetus in the new composition or variation, serve us well. To quote Genette: 'In music, the range of transformational possibilities is probably broader than in painting, broader than in literature certainly, given the complexity of musical discourse, which, unlike the literary text, is unhampered by the strict "linearity" of the verbal signifier' (1997 [1982]: 386). Chapter 2 explores further the potential for phrases appropriated from the discipline of music and musicology, terms such as variation and sampling, for example, to revivify our understandings of the kinetic processes of adaptation.

As this endless ruminating over terminology suggests, this is a study sympathetic to pluralism rather than fixity. To this end, the volume is divided into three parts. The first section 'Defining Terms' offers a series of definitions for, and ways of thinking about, adaptation and appropriation as practice and process. The aim is to open out and widen the range of terms and their applications, rather than fixing or ossifying specific concepts of adaptation and appropriation. The second section on 'Literary Archetypes' examines the recurring interest of adaptation and appropriation in many of the central texts of Western culture: myth, fairy tale and folklore, and Shakespeare. The latter playwright, of course, reworks in his texts many of the structures and storylines of myth and fairy tale, indicating the cultural osmosis that regularly occurs between adaptive writers and texts. It will be witnessed in this study how frequently adaptations adapt other adaptations. There is a filtration effect taking place, a cross-pollination; we are observing mediations through culture, practice, and history that cannot be underestimated. The final section widens the parameters yet further, considering the 'Alternative Perspectives' offered by adaptations and appropriations. As well as exploring specific re-visions of canonical texts by William Shakespeare, Daniel Defoe, Charlotte Brontë, and Virginia Woolf, this section considers the ongoing interest in recreating and critiquing the Victorian era in various acts of reworking and pastiche, not least in the field of prose fiction. From a detailed focus on appropriations of fictional writing, the latter chapters of the volume consider the appropriation of historical 'fact', and the adaptation of alternative art forms in the domain of the literary and the cinematic.

What becomes clear as these sections progress is how frequently adaptations and appropriations are impacted upon by movements in, and readings produced by, the theoretical and intellectual arena as much as by their so-called sources. Many of the texts and films studied here are produced as much by the tenets of feminism, poststructuralism, postcolonialism, queer theory, and postmodernism as by the literary canon *per se*. As the critical anxieties and the Robert Weimann quotation at the beginning of this introduction indicated, the reproductive capacity of appropriation and the study of appropriation cannot be underestimated. Texts feed off each other and create other texts, and other critical studies; literature creates other literature. Part of the sheer pleasure of the reading experience must be the tension between the familiar and the new, and the recognition both of similarity and difference, between ourselves and between texts. The pleasure exists, and persists, then, in the act of reading in, around, and on (and on).

PART 1

DEFINING TERMS

1

WHAT IS ADAPTATION?

All matter is transformed into other matter.

Kate Atkinson, *Not the End of the World*

The processes of adaptation and appropriation that are the concern of this book are in many respects a sub-section of the over-arching practice of intertextuality. As mentioned in the introduction, the notion of intertextuality is most readily associated with Julia Kristeva who, invoking examples from literature, art, and music, made the case in essays such as 'The Bounded Text' (1980) and 'Word, Dialogue, Novel' (1986) that all texts invoke and rework other texts in a rich and ever-evolving cultural mosaic. The impulse towards intertextuality, and the narrative and architectural *bricolage* that can result from that impulse, is regarded by many as a central tenet of postmodernism (Allen 2000).

The interleaving of different texts and textual traditions, which is manifest in the intertextual impulse, has also been linked to the postcolonial notion of 'hybridity'. Homi Bhabha's account of hybridity suggests how things and ideas are 'repeated, relocated and translated in the name of tradition' (1995: 207), but also how this process of relocation can stimulate new utterances and creativity. For Bhabha, however, only hybridity that respects essential difference enables innovation, whereas the cultural synthesis or homogenization of multiculturalism proves stifling (208). Science-led notions of hybridization regard cultural artefacts as irrevocably changed by the process of interaction. In the case of post-colonial cultures this is particularly problematic, since if the scientific notion of dominant and recessive factors (or genes) holds true for cultures, then the colonial or imperial tradition dominates over the indigenous in any hybridized form. This notion of the dominant and the recessive was an idea first posited by the scientific experimenter in patterns of heredity, Gregor Mendel, in the mid-nineteenth century (Tudge 2002), but in the literary field it has been adopted to articulate a debate about dominance and suppression that is crucial for any consideration of intertextual relationships.

Studies of adaptation and appropriation intersect in this way not only with the scientific idiom, which T. S. Eliot deployed in his essay 'Tradition and the Individual Talent' when he wrote of the chemical reaction between literary inheritance and the artist that created a wholly new 'compound' (Eliot 1984: 41), but also with the critical and cultural movements of postmodernism and postcolonialism; indeed, the effort to write a history of adaptation necessarily transmutes at various points into a history of critical theory. As well as throwing up potent theoretical intertexts of their own, adaptation studies mobilize a wide vocabulary of active terms: version, variation, interpretation, continuation, transformation, imitation, pastiche, parody, forgery, travesty, transposition, revaluation, revision, rewriting, echo. As this list of terms suggests, adaptations and appropriations can possess starkly different, even opposing, aims and intentions; as a result, adaptation studies often favour a kind of 'open structuralism' along the lines proposed by Gérard Genette in *Palimpsests* (1997: ix), readings which are invested not in proving a text's closure to alternatives, but in celebrating its ongoing interaction with other texts and artistic productions. To this end, sequels, prequels, compression, and amplification all have a role to play at different times in the adaptive mode.

Adaptation can be a transpositional practice, casting a specific genre into another generic mode, an act of re-vision in itself. It can parallel editorial practice in some respects, indulging in the exercise of trimming and pruning; yet it can also be an amplificatory procedure engaged in addition, expansion, accretion, and interpolation (compare, for example, Deppman *et al.* 2004 on 'genetic criticism'). Adaptation is frequently involved in offering commentary on a sourcetext. This is achieved most often by offering a revised point of view from the 'original', adding hypothetical motivation, or voicing the silenced and marginalized. Yet adaptation can also constitute a simpler attempt to make texts 'relevant' or easily comprehensible to new audiences and readerships via the processes of proximation and updating. This can be seen as an artistic drive in many adaptations of so-called 'classic' novels or drama for television and cinema. Shakespeare has been a particular focus, a beneficiary even, of these 'proximations' or updatings.

The relevance of particular terms to a specific text, and the moment in time when they become active, can provide some very specific clues to a text's possible meanings and its cultural impact, intended or otherwise. As Robert Weimann stresses, appropriation as an activity 'is not closed to the forces of social struggle and political power or to acts of historical consciousness' (1988: 433). The intention here is to examine in detail the specific impulses and ideologies, personal and historical, that are at play in various acts of adaptation and appropriation. It seems useful therefore to start by unpacking in some detail what we might mean by such umbrella terms and considering the different modes and methodologies of adaptation, as well as its varying disciplinary manifestations.

In his richly informative study of 'hypertextuality', Genette described the act of writing a text, in whatever genre, with other texts in mind as a 'transgeneric practice'. As any reading of this book will make clear, a vast range of genres and sub-genres are regularly involved in the kind of hypertextual activities Genette interrogates. Adaptation is, however, frequently a specific process involving the transition from one genre to another: novels into film; drama into musical; the dramatization of prose narrative and prose fiction; or the inverse movement of making drama into prose narrative.

We have already established that when we discuss adaptation in these pages we are often working with reinterpretations of established texts in new generic contexts or perhaps with relocations of an 'original' or sourcetext's cultural and/or temporal setting, which may or may not involve a generic shift. Modules on higher education programmes which examine the transition of literature into film are fairly commonplace these days and any student engaged in such work is implicitly, if not explicitly, studying adaptation, thinking critically about what it means to adapt or appropriate. Intellectual or scholarly examinations of this kind are not aimed at identifying 'good' or 'bad' adaptations. On what grounds, after all, could such a judgement be made? Fidelity to the original? As I hope this volume indicates, it is usually at the very point of infidelity that the most creative acts of adaptation and appropriation take place. The sheer possibility of testing fidelity in any tangible way is surely also in question when we are dealing with such labile texts as Shakespeare's plays. Adaptation studies are, then, not about making polarized value judgements, but about analysing process, ideology, and methodology.

Establishing some useful templates for studying cinematic interpretations of well-known novels, Deborah Cartmell argues for three broad categories of adaptation:

(i)   transposition
(ii) commentary
(iii) analogue

(Cartmell and Whelehan 1999: 24)

On the surface, all screen versions of novels are transpositions in the sense that they take a text from one genre and deliver it to new audiences by means of the aesthetic conventions of an entirely different generic process (here novel into film). But many adaptations, of novels and other generic forms, contain further layers of transposition, relocating their source texts not just generically, but in cultural, geographical and temporal terms. Baz Luhrmann's 1996 *William Shakespeare's Romeo + Juliet* is a useful example: updating Shakespeare's early modern Veronese tragedy to a contemporary North American setting, Luhrmann retains the playtext's sense of urban gang feuding but accords it a troublingly immediate and topical resonance. Famously, the much-mentioned swords and rapiers of Shakespeare's playscript become in Luhrmann's vividly realized Verona Beach the engraved monikers for the modern era's weapon of choice, the handgun. Genette would describe this as a 'movement of proximation' (1997: 304), and it is extremely common in screen adaptations of classic novels.

As mentioned, Shakespeare's *oeuvre* has proven to be a particularly rich seam to mine for such proximations: in 1999 Kenneth Branagh remade *Love's Labour's Lost* as a 1930s Hollywood film musical, embedding Shakespeare's competition of courtly wit and sonneteering within a *faux*-Oxbridge context. The events of the film unfurled on the eve of the Second World War, providing its audiences with a more recent historical context of conflict than the Shakespearean play's interaction with the late sixteenth-century French Wars of Religion, and Branagh added a deliberately nostalgic soundtrack of songs by George and Ira Gershwin and Cole Porter to appeal to those members of the audience who shared that cultural memory. Michael Almereyda's millennial *Hamlet* re-envisioned Elsinore as a Manhattan financial corporation with Claudius as a corrupt CEO (2000). In an interesting twist, the disaffected young prince in this version was an anti-establishment art student, who created his 'play within a play' as a video montage to be submitted as a course assignment. The motive behind updating is fairly obvious: the 'movement of proximation' brings it closer to the audience's frame of reference in temporal, geographic, or social terms. Not all transpositional adaptations that make temporal shifts move forward to a date nearer the present – Franco Zeffirelli's 1990 film *Hamlet*, for example, opted for a Gothic medieval setting – but it is certainly the most common approach. In the example of Zeffirelli's *Hamlet* it could be argued that his casting was an implicit updating since it brought to bear a self-conscious act of intertextuality with the world of film action heroes, in particular the specific brand represented by his Hamlet, Mel Gibson.

Shakespeare is not the sole focus of transpositional adaptation, although, as we will witness in Chapter 3, his works do provide a cultural barometer for the historically contingent process of adaptation. In 1998, director Alfonso Cuarón effected a similar shift of setting and context with Charles Dickens's Bildungsroman, *Great Expectations*, relocating it to contemporary New York, with his Pip (Finn Bell) as a struggling artist. Comparable transpositions can be found of the work of Henrik Ibsen, Jane Austen and Anton Chekhov, among others.

There is a case to be made that in some instances the process of adaptation starts to move away from simple proximation towards something more culturally loaded. This constitutes Cartmell's second category: commentary, or adaptations that comment on the politics of the source text, or those of the new *mise-en-scène*, or both, usually by means of alteration or addition. Film versions of Shakespeare's *The Tempest*, for example, which bring the Algerian witch Sycorax visibly onscreen, comment by means of this action on her absence from the play. In Shakespeare's text she is constructed solely by means of Prospero's negative word-portraits. Derek Jarman's 1979 film *The Tempest* and Peter Greenaway's lush epic *Prospero's Books* (1991) both featured an onscreen Sycorax. One film version of Jane Austen's *Mansfield Park* (dir. Patricia Rozema, 2000) made explicit that novel's context in the history of British colonialism and the practice of slavery on Antiguan plantations. Rozema made visible facts that the novel represses. In both these instances, the absence or gap in the original narrative being remarked upon in the transpositional film was one that had been identified by postcolonial criticism.

It could be argued that in all these examples the full impact of the film adaptation depends upon the audience's awareness of an explicit relationship to a source text. In expectation of this most formal adaptations carry the same title as their source text. The desire to make the relationship with the source explicit links to the manner in which the responses to adaptations depend upon a complex invocation of ideas of similarity and difference. These ideas can only be mobilized by a reader or spectator alert to the intertextual relationship, and this in turn requires the deployment of well-known texts or sources. Philip Cox has suggested as much in relation to the huge popularity of stage adaptations of Charles Dickens's novels in the nineteenth century. These productions consciously staged tableaux, images re-enacting famous moments from the novels: 'The use of the illustration-tableau would suggest the expectation of audience familiarity with the serial instalments of the novels themselves: the pleasure to be gained through such acts of mimicry could only be brought about by an instant recognition of the similarities' (2000: 43–4). It is, of course, in this way that adaptations and appropriations prove complicit in activating and reactivating the canonical status of certain texts and writers, even when the more politicized appropriation may be seeking to challenge that very status.

In Cartmell's third and final category of adaptation, analogue, the case is rather different. While it may enrich and deepen our understanding of the new cultural product to be aware of its shaping intertext, it may not be entirely necessary to enjoy the work independently: recent examples of stand-alone works that nevertheless deepen when their status as analogue is revealed might include: Amy Heckerling's *Clueless*, a Valley-Girl variation on Jane Austen's *Emma* (1995); Francis Ford

Coppola's Vietnam film *Apocalypse Now* (1979) and its recontextualization of Joseph Conrad's dark nineteenth-century exploration of the colonial enterprise in the Congo, *Heart of Darkness*; and Michael Winterbottom's *The Claim* (2001), in which Thomas Hardy's *The Mayor of Casterbridge* is re-envisioned as a subtle variation on the Hollywood genre of the Western, relocating the action to gold-rush America in the 1860s. Another example which actually exhibits a two-stage process of adaptation and absorption is William Reilly's *Men of Respect* (1990), a late twentieth-century US film about the Mafia, which reworks both a 1955 film about the British gangland scene, *Joe Macbeth* (dir. Ken Hughes) and that film's own Shakespearean dramatic precursor, *Macbeth*. The complex question provoked by these examples as to whether or not knowledge of a source text is required or merely enriching will recur throughout the readings proffered in this volume.

It would, of course, be misleading to apply adaptation studies solely to cinematic versions of canonical plays and novels, although that is perhaps its most common and easily understood manifestation. Another genre that is engaged in self-conscious adaptation on a regular basis is the stage and film musical. Intriguingly, Shakespeare once again appears as a facilitating presence: as well as *The Boys from Syracuse* which made *The Comedy of Errors* into a musical, there is Jerome Robbins's and Robert Wise's *West Side Story*, with music by Leonard Bernstein, which re-envisioned *Romeo and Juliet* as a 1950s tale of gang violence in the streets and concrete playgrounds of New York. This in turn influenced Luhrmann's 1996 film adaptation of Shakespeare's romantic tragedy. *Kiss Me Kate* famously riffs on *The Taming of the Shrew*, by means of the songs of Cole Porter. Porter's involvement in this earlier Shakespearean adaptation was clearly an informing influence for Branagh when 'updating' *Love's Labour's Lost* in 1999.

The musical finds much of its source material in the literary canon: from Victor Hugo's epic novel *Les Misérables* to T. S. Eliot's *Old Possum's Book of Practical Cats*. One musical which has achieved its own canonical status is *My Fair Lady*, a version of George Bernard Shaw's play *Pygmalion*, which in its title glances even further back into the literary past for its influences, to the shape-shifting stories of Ovid's *Metamorphoses* where Pygmalion creates a statue with which he falls in love. We will explore other Ovidian adaptations in Chapter 4, but what already begins to emerge is the more kinetic account of adaptation and appropriation that we were arguing for in the Introduction: these texts rework texts that often themselves reworked texts. The process of adaptation is constant and ongoing.

It is not entirely unconnected that the disciplinary domains in which the term 'adaptation' has proved most resonant are biology and ecology. Following Charles Darwin's presentation of his controversial theories of evolution in the nineteenth century, the scientific community has been endlessly fascinated with the complex processes of environmental and genetic adaptation, from Darwin's famous finches on the Galapagos islands, whose variations in bill and beak type were an indicator of the different foodstuffs they had adapted to eat in competition with one another, to the peppered moth in British industrial cities, a melanism or darker variation on the traditional species thought to have developed to blend in with the blackened surfaces caused by heavy industry in those areas. Adaptation proves in these examples to be a far from neutral, indeed highly active, mode of being, far removed from the unimaginative act of imitation, copying, or repetition that it is sometimes presented as being by literature and film critics obsessed with claims to 'originality'. Adaptation and appropriation also provide their own intertexts, so that adaptations perform in dialogue with other adaptations as well as their informing source. Perhaps it serves us better to think in terms of complex processes of filtration, and in terms of intertextual webs or signifying fields, rather than simplistic one-way lines of influence from source to adaptation.

In all of these categorizations and definitions of adaptation, it remains crucial that we keep in sight the pleasure principle. In a very suggestive account of film's impact upon our experience of canonical literature, John Ellis argues that adaptation enables a prolonging or extension of pleasure connected to memory: 'Adaptation into another medium becomes a means of prolonging the pleasure of the original presentation, and repeating the production of a memory' (1982: 4–5). Ellis's thesis is, of course, equally resonant in its application to the recent vogue for television adaptations of classic texts, best exemplified by the genre of the BBC period drama in the UK: examples include adaptations of Jane Austen's *Pride and Prejudice*, Elizabeth Gaskell's *North and South*, and George Eliot's *Daniel Deronda*, although the practice also extends beyond the realms of the nineteenth-century novel and into the domain of contemporary fiction with the recent three-part adaptation of Jonathan Coe's *The Rotters' Club*, which proved as much a loving reconstruction of a particular historical era or period, in this case the decade of the 1970s, as any of the previous examples.

By prolonging the pleasure of the initial act of reading or the initial encounter with a text, Ellis suggests that 'adaptation trades upon the memory of the novel, a memory that can derive from actual reading, or, as is more likely with a classic of literature, a generally circulated memory' (3). He continues, 'This adaptation consumes this memory, attempting to efface it with the presence of its own images' (3). It is at this point that I part company with his otherwise persuasive argument. For consumption need not always be the intended endpoint of adaptation; the adapting text does not necessarily seek to consume or efface the informing source. Indeed, as I will suggest in these pages, it is the very endurance and survival of the source text that enables the ongoing process of juxtaposed readings that are crucial to the cultural operations of adaptation, and the ongoing experiences of pleasure for the reader or spectator in tracing the intertextual relationships. It is this inherent sense of play, produced in part by the activation of our informed sense of similarity and difference between the texts being invoked, and the connected interplay of expectation and surprise, that for me lies at the heart of the experience of adaptation and appropriation.

2

WHAT IS APPROPRIATION?

There are many ways in which both the practice and the effects of adaptation and appropriation intersect and interrelate, yet it is equally important to maintain some clear distinctions between them as creative activities. An adaptation signals a relationship with an informing sourcetext or original; a cinematic version of Shakespeare's *Hamlet*, for example, although clearly reinterpreted by the collaborative efforts of director, scriptwriter, actors, and the generic demands of the movement from stage drama to film, remains ostensibly *Hamlet*, a specific version, albeit achieved in alternative temporal and generic modes, of that seminal cultural text. On the other hand, appropriation frequently affects a more decisive journey away from the informing source into a wholly new cultural product and domain. This may or may not involve a generic shift, and it may still require the intellectual juxtaposition of (at least) one text against another that we have suggested is central to the reading and spectating experience of adaptations. But the appropriated text or texts are not always as clearly signalled or acknowledged as in the adaptive process. They may occur in a far less straightforward context than is evident in making a film version of a canonical play. This chapter aims to unpack some of the diverse modes and operations of appropriation. To ease discussion, the examples have been divided into two broad categories: embedded texts and sustained appropriations.

EMBEDDED TEXTS AND INTERPLAY

The stage and film musical has already been cited as an inherently adaptational form, often reworking canonical plays, poems, and novels into a mode that deploys song and dance to deliver its narrative. *West Side Story* and *Kiss Me Kate*, two previously mentioned Shakespeare-informed musicals, are interesting examples of the practice since they go one stage further than the generic adaptation involved in making Victor Hugo's *Les Misérables* or George Bernard Shaw's *Pygmalion* into a musically-based performance. *West Side Story* would not exist without *Romeo and Juliet*: Tony and Maria are clearly modern reworkings of Shakespeare's 'star-crossed' protagonists in a 1950s New York context. Their story of a love denied by feuding urban communities, and in particular the two gangs, the Jets and the Sharks, clearly has its origins in the Montague-Capulet rivalry, the 'ancient grudge' that drives the prejudice and violence of Shakespeare's stage Verona. This carefully realized *mise-en-scène* highlighted what was a topical issue of race conflict in New York at the time when the musical was first written and performed: resentment of and violence towards the immigrant Puerto Rican community.

There is much pleasure to be had in tracing the relationships and overlaps between the two texts. The iconic fire escapes of the West Side provide a brilliant counterpart to the balcony scene of Shakespeare's playtext. Romeo's quasi-patriarch and confidante, the Friar, first seen in the play collecting herbs, is transformed into gentle 'Doc', owner of the local drugstore where many of the Jets meet. In a production working in a 'teenage' idiom and context, the late 1950s being the moment when teenage culture was formalized in both cultural and commercial terms, 'Doc' is the sole parental figure we see on stage or screen (the musical was made into a film in 1961). Maria's parents are heard, but only as voices off; authority is effectively evacuated from the stage. There are other supposed figures of authority present onstage in the shape of Officer Krupke and his colleagues from the NYPD, but they are laughably corrupt and ineffectual in their handling of the tense situation on the streets they police. In Shakespeare's play, Juliet has a counterpart confidante to Romeo's in the comic body of the Nurse. In *West Side Story* the comic aspect of this relationship is downplayed in favour of the sisterly attentions of Anita, fiancée to Maria's gangleader brother Bernardo. One sequence depicts an unforgettable choreographed gang rape; we witness Anita enduring this at the hands of the Jets when she tries, and fails, to deliver Maria's message to Tony. This is another suggestive reading and reworking of the play, both of Mercutio's bawdy misogynistic banter with the Nurse and the misdelivered letter that Jacques Derrida and others have identified as the crucial turning point of *Romeo and Juliet* (Derrida 1992: 419).

This is adaptation, then, but it is adaptation in another mode. *West Side Story* can and does stand alone as a musical in its own right, without need of the *Romeo and Juliet* connection, although I would still maintain that for audiences of the musical an intertextual awareness deepens and enriches the range of possible responses. Lyrics such as 'There's a place for us' undoubtedly return us to issues of spatial confinement in the original play; and the Jets' much reiterated gang tag 'Womb to Tomb' evokes the tragic confinement of possibility for the play's young protagonists whose love is consummated only in the face of death and ultimately, literally, in the encasement of the Capulet family tomb. This is a fine example of the more sustained reworking of the source text which we have identified as intrinsic to appropriation: rather than the movements of proximation or cross-generic interpretation that we identified as central to adaptation, here we have a wholesale rethinking of the terms of the original.

Kiss Me Kate has Shakespeare's misogynistic comedy *The Taming of the Shrew* quite literally at its core: in a classic metatheatrical move, the musical (filmed in 1953) is about a group of performers staging a musical version of *The Taming of the Shrew*. Audiences register two levels of adaptation and appropriation. The embedded '*The Shrew*' musical is a more straightforward adaptation, along the lines we were establishing in Chapter 1, reworking the characters and events of Shakespeare's play in a song and dance format. As a result many of the central songs, including 'I Hate Men', derive from the musical-within-the-musical. That format is itself quasi-Shakespearean, recalling the plays-within-a-play of, among others, *Hamlet*, *Love's Labour's Lost*, and *A Midsummer Night's Dream*, but, of course, most appositely recalling the metatheatrical framework of *The Taming of the Shrew* itself. *Shrew* opens with the 'Induction', which establishes that the whole play of Katherina and Petruchio's embattled relationship is a performance by a troupe of travelling actors who have tricked the inebriated Christopher Sly into thinking he is a lord watching household theatricals on his aristocratic estate. *Kiss Me Kate* frames its *Shrew* musical with a plotline of embattled theatre stars, once married but now divorced. There are obvious, hilarious ways in which their offstage temperaments mirror their onstage performances; Lilli Vanessi, for example, is outspoken and hotheaded in a manner akin to her character Katherina. While the musical's untroubled manifestations of early twentieth-century US sexual politics, including the beatings and confinements visited upon the forceful Lilli, may no longer seem so amusing in an era alert to domestic violence, the point remains that *Kiss Me Kate* is both adaptation and appropriation at the same time. If the pure adaptation rests in the embedded musical, then the appropriative aspect is found in the wider framework story of the US theatre performers and in the related subplot of the Mafia henchmen seeking debt repayment from the production's Hortensio, Bill Calhoun. The gangsters deliver one of the show's most famous songs, whose title has itself almost reached the status of comic by-line for the act of Shakespearean appropriation: 'Brush up Your Shakespeare'. When Angela Carter chose this as one of three epigraphs to her late novel on theatre, Shakespeare, and musical, *Wise Children* (1992), she was anticipating a readership with a vivid cultural memory of *Kiss Me Kate*.

Kiss Me Kate can obviously be viewed and understood in the context of Shakespearean appropriation more generally, which, as we will see in Chapter 3, is a veritable cultural field in its own right, but it also relates to a tradition of what can best be described as 'backstage dramas'. These are texts interested in going behind the scenes of performances of particular plays or shows. This can be achieved in a self-reflexive way on the stage, as in *Kiss Me Kate* or Michael Frayn's play about English repertory theatre, *Noises Off*. *Shakespeare in Love* (dir. John Madden, 1998) also exploits this motif, exploring an offstage relationship between Will Shakespeare and his star performer Thomas Kent (a disguised Viola de Lesseps) via suggestive cinematic cross-cutting between their 'real' life and their onstage performance in *Romeo and Juliet*.

Backstage drama of this kind has also been developed in a prose fiction context. Australian author Thomas Keneally's 1987 novel *The Playmaker* recounts the rehearsals and performance of a production of George Farquhar's 1706 play *The Recruiting Officer*. The play is performed by a group of convict actors, who have been assembled for the purpose by Lieutenant Ralph Clark, a British military officer involved in overseeing the penal colony established in Sydney, Australia in the late eighteenth century. In a funny and touching account of the rehearsal period, Keneally draws on resonant echoes between the events of Farquhar's play, which depicts the sexual shenanigans of a group of recruiting officers in the provincial shire town of Shrewsbury, and daily life in the penal colony where site-specific hierarchies prevail and where many of the women convicts are the sexual property of the military officers and overseers. Lieutenant Clark falls in love with his lead actor, Mary Brenham, a convicted clothes thief who performs the part of the cross-dressing Silvia in Farquhar's comedy, but we are always aware of the geographical and temporal parameters to this love-story. In the epilogue to the novel – Keneally structures his narrative in the form of five chapters and an epilogue, self-consciously recalling dramatic structure – we learn of Ralph's return to his English fiancée. Mary Brenham, as with the majority of the convicts whose lives we have followed, simply slips from the historical record. Keneally's purpose in writing this novel has relevance far beyond the 1789 setting of the events it purports to recall; shadowing the world of the penal community represented in the novel stand the lives of the displaced aboriginal communities of Australia. For all the play-within-the-novel's claims to be the 'first' theatre production in this 'new' land, the reader is made all too aware that the Sydney penal colony is far from being the 'original' existence on the island. Behind his surface appropriation of Farquhar's play to explore the penal colony (Keneally also worked extensively with historical records of the same), the author is concerned with another more hostile and imperialist act of cultural appropriation: the seizure of the land rights and cultural claims of the aboriginal peoples. The novel is dedicated to 'Arabanoo and his brethren, still dispossessed', and Keneally has continued to be a prominent campaigner against Australia's current restrictive immigration laws. Appropriation then, as with adaptation, shades in important ways into the discursive domains of other disciplines, in particular here the legal discourse surrounding the controversial areas of land and property rights.

Intriguingly, Keneally's novel underwent a further process of adaptation when playwright Timberlake Wertenbaker recreated it as a stage drama, *Our Country's Good*, in 1988. Following the practice of adaptation outlined in the previous chapter, Wertenbaker altered, condensed, and redirected the focus of Keneally's novel. She chose to commence the play with a scene on board the convict ship transporting the prisoners to Australia, whereas in the novel this is only ever recalled in flashback and by means of shared memories. Adding the specific character, and in some sense mouthpiece, of the Governor-in-Chief of New South Wales, Arthur Phillip, Wertenbaker embeds in her play several extended justifications for the rehabilitative and socially constructive power of the arts in general, and of theatre in particular. She had her own political motives for doing so in the late 1980s. The debates conducted in the play about the social and cultural importance of the arts had a highly topical resonance in an era of UK Arts Council funding cuts. In an interesting twist, *Our Country's Good* has in turn proved an extremely popular play for staging and performance by prison drama groups. These acting companies find personal resonance in the playscript. Reading the available accounts of several prison actors of the inspirational effect of the artistic experience of staging *Our Country's Good*, there exists a sense in which the events described in Keneally's novel have travelled full circle (Wertenbaker 1991 [1988]: vi-xvi).

Wertenbaker's play was first staged by the Royal Court Theatre Company in London, playing in repertory alongside *The Recruiting Officer*. To emphasize the connections further, both productions involved the same company of actors. On one night audiences could see a particular actor playing Justice Balance in *The Recruiting Officer* and then the next day that same actor playing Ketch Freeman in *Our Country's Good*, the public hangman who assumes the role of Balance in the Australian convict production. Those spectators who saw both plays in quick succession were being invited to make their content and material play off against one another, just as they do in Keneally's founding novel.

Another double-hander frequently staged by theatre companies for related reasons and with similar effects is Alan Ayckbourn's *A Chorus of Disapproval*. This play is also about a theatre company rehearsing a production, this time a provincial British theatre company. The company is staging an amateur operatic production of John Gay's eighteenth-century musical *The Beggars' Opera*. Gay's text has been subject to numerous cultural adaptations and acts of filtration, famously providing the template for Bertolt Brecht's *Threepenny Opera*. Ayckbourn ensures that his audiences are alert to the particular connection between his play and Gay's by commencing *A Chorus of Disapproval* at the end as it were, as the curtain falls on the successful performance and the actors take their bows. As a consequence of this, when the play launches back in time to the start of the audition and rehearsal process the audience knows it is tracing Guy Jones's ascent from theatre hopeful into leading man. Of course, the humour resides in the fact that Guy becomes too identified with his part as Gay's womanizing criminal protagonist Macheath, upsetting various female members of the company in the process. Much of the comedy of *A Chorus of Disapproval* derives from an audience's active engagement with the embedded text of *The Beggars' Opera*, playing on similarity and difference yet again. Ayckbourn highlights the continuity of actor and part but also the discontinuities between his privileged provincial setting and the eighteenth-century underworld of Gay's comic opera. When Gay's musical drama plays in repertory with Ayckbourn's play, these connections and contrasts become even more pertinent for audiences.

Encouraged interplay between appropriations and their sources begins to emerge, then, as a fundamental, even vital, aspect of the reading or spectating experience, one productive of new meanings, applications, and resonance. But, as already stressed, appropriation does not always make its founding relationships and interrelationships as clear as these plays with named, embedded texts. The gesture towards the source text(s) can be wholly more shadowy than in these explicit situations, and this brings into play, sometimes in controversial ways, questions of intellectual property, proper acknowledgement, and, at its worse, the charge of plagiarism.

SUSTAINED APPROPRIATION: HOMAGE OR PLAGIARISM?

When Graham Swift won the Booker Prize in 1996 for his novel *Last Orders*, a controversy over the award soon emerged. As Pamela Cooper has recorded, connections were identified between Swift's novel and William Faulkner's 1930 American classic *As I Lay Dying*:

> In a letter to the book review supplement of the newspaper *The Australian*, John Flow of the University of Queensland underlined

some very close similarities in structure and subject-matter, including a monologue given to the dead person, a monologue consisting of numbered points, and a monologue made up of a single sentence.

(Cooper 2002: 17)

Flow's accusation was that this provable line of influence from Faulkner rendered Swift's book a substandard derivation of *As I Lay Dying* and therefore unworthy of a prize for which the judges' commendation had drawn attention to the book's originality. Charges and counter-charges flew in the British press with several Booker judges, including Jonathan Coe, admitting that they had never read the Faulkner book (Cooper 2002: 60), and Julian Barnes defending Swift on the grounds that borrowing and appropriation were a standard feature of the artistic process. Swift himself called *Last Orders* an 'homage' to Faulkner, and it should be stressed that earlier work by him had been compared to Faulkner's writing, not least *Waterland* (1983) in the way that it approached land as character. As Flow's critique of *Last Orders* made explicit, there are notable structural overlaps between Faulkner's tale of a Mississippi family group transporting the corpse of their dead wife/mother to the town of Jefferson for burial and Swift's story of four male friends transporting the ashes of their late friend, the butcher Jack Dodds, to scatter off the end of Margate Pier.

Faulkner's novel is shaped by means of a series of juxtaposed monologues, both from family members, including the highly poetic but increasingly mentally estranged Darl, who in some sense provides the novel's central narrative consciousness, and who is ironically incarcerated in an asylum by the close, and onlookers to the grotesque comedy of the strongly smelling coffin being carried through floods and townships en route to its final resting place. At one point we have a single sentence monologue from one character in the Faulkner novel – the child Vardaman – and by comparison Swift has Vince's exclamation of 'Old buggers' while at the Chatham naval war memorial (Swift 1996: 130). Faulkner's corpse, Addie Bundren, speaks a single monologue, delivered as it were from beyond the grave, as does Swift's Jack Dodds (285). In both novels, readers are party to the monologues of women left behind: Cora Tull in *As I Lay Dying* and Amy, Jack's widow, in *Last Orders*. In one remarkable sequence in the Faulkner narrative, Cash, the eldest Bundren son, recounts the almost obsessive care with which he fashioned the coffin in which his mother's rotting corpse is now being transported; the nailing together of the coffin is the action and sound that promulgates and defines the opening of the novel. In *Last Orders* this section has been transformed into Ray Johnson's 'rules' for betting on horses. In both novels, these lists have a metaphorical application to life. In a manner similar to Faulkner's Darl and Cash, whose two very distinct voices and world-views – Darl's poetic and sensitive but vulnerable to complete fragmentation and collapse, Cash's pragmatic and prosaic, although highly perceptive – provide the central juxtaposed narratives of *As I Lay Dying*, Ray's monologues in *Last Orders* present him as the central consciousness in Swift's text. Between the gaps or lines of Ray's narrative, we learn of his love for Jack's wife Amy, and his estrangement from his own wife and daughter, as well as the past history of this complicated set of friends and associates (many of the relationships date from 1940s wartime experiences).

What is both interesting and troubling in the case of *Last Orders* and the 'homage' to Faulkner is that what in studies of Shakespeare might be termed an examination of sources or creative borrowings, citing allusions to or redeployments of Ovid, Plutarch, Thomas Lodge, the Roman comedies and so on, becomes in the case of a modern novel a reductive discussion of plagiarism and 'inauthenticity'. Robert Weimann gestures at this point in his observation that: 'In precapitalist societies the distance between the poet's act of appropriating a given text or theme and his or her own intellectual product and property is much smaller: the extent to which his *matière* is given, the extent to which "source", genre, plot patterns, topoi, and so on are pre-ordained is much greater ...' (1988: 434). This is a Marxist-inflected questioning of property and 'ownership' at its heart, but it is worth adding that in his volume on *Literature* in this series, Peter Widdowson asserted that 'revisionary' writing is a fundamental sub-set of what we might categorize as the literary (1999).

The consonances between the two works, Faulkner's and Swift's, are inescapable but what is of particular interest in the context of this volume is the specific charge of indebtedness that was being made by Flow and others. Flow seemed to suggest that Swift's novel was devalued because it was not 'original', an unsustainable argument in the context of a postmodern culture of borrowings and *bricolage*. But what also concerned many of the critics and readers who responded to Flow's charge was the idea that Swift had somehow been intellectually dishonest by reworking Faulkner's remarkable novel into a late twentieth-century and vernacular English idiom without paying due acknowledgement. Would *Last Orders* have regained cultural status if, in a prefatory note, Swift had explicitly recorded his debt, or openly declared his intentional homage? Should his novel's title have indicated its intertextual relationship in the way that Joyce's *Ulysses* does its interaction with Homeric epic? Yet Joyce's novel is also linked to Shakespeare's *Hamlet* but the 1922 novel bears no trace of that relationship in its title. Does that make it somehow dishonest, less worthy in literary terms, less *original*? Surely not. The response to *Last Orders* raises the important question as to whether a novelist needs to 'adequately' acknowledge intertextuality and allusiveness. If we adhere to some of Genette's theories of palimpsestuous writing discussed in the previous chapter, surely part of the pleasure of response for the reader consists in tracing those relationships for themselves. Without wishing to reduce the act of reading to a game of 'spot the appropriation' it is surely important to acknowledge that to tie an adaptive and appropriative text to one sole intertext may in fact close down the opportunity to read it in relationship with others. This is certainly true of *Last Orders*.

Swift's novel is in many respects all about the search for family and a sense of home, and, like so many novels of travel, its ultimate focus is on the starting point rather than any notional destination. Swift is appropriating several literary archetypes in this respect. The device of the journey is ancient and archetypal in Western and other literatures, as is the topic of death. As Swift has registered: 'The story about the pressure of the dead on the living, in the wake of death, is as old as Homer' (Cited in Cooper 2002: 17). Swift has always been a deeply allusive writer. *Waterland* opens with a suggestive epigraph from Dickens's *Great Expectations*: 'Ours was the marsh country ...'; *Ever After* (1992) carries resonances of *Hamlet*, as discussed in Chapter 3; and, as invoked in Chapter 4, *The Light of Day* (2003) rewrites the genre of detective fiction, alluding in the process both to Graham Greene's *The End of the Affair* and the classical myth of Orpheus. Pamela Cooper has identified further links between *Last Orders* and the poetry of T. S. Eliot, in particular 'The Waste Land' with its London public house refrain of 'Time gentlemen please'. Of course, Eliot's poem has several rich intertexts of its own, but one which strikes the reader early on is that of Geoffrey Chaucer's seminal medieval work, *The Canterbury Tales*, whose positive hopeful opening in spring: 'Whan that Aprill with his shoures soote / The droghte of March hath perced to the roote' (Chaucer 1986: General Prologue, ll. 1–16), Eliot inverts to 'April is the cruellest month'. This invocation in turn alerts us to a parallel set of allusions in Swift's novel to Chaucer's story of pilgrimage. The narrative appears to enjoy alerting the reader to the intertextual game: 'Look out for signs to Canterbury' (181). There is even a significant detour into Canterbury Cathedral.

By appropriating Chaucer's *Canterbury Tales*, Swift adopts and adapts the ancient literary strategy of paralleling actual journey or place-pilgrimage with inner journey or spiritual travel. These themes and the Chaucerian intertext are all glancingly alluded to in the opening pages of *Last Orders*. Ray is sitting in a Bermondsey public house – the jokingly named 'Coach and Horses' since, as the characters keep reflecting, 'it aint never gone nowhere' (6) – which of course parallels the Southwark inn, the Tabard, in which Chaucer's twenty-nine pilgrims first encounter one another and decide to travel together, passing the time by telling stories at the suggestion and behest of Harry Bailey, the Host. Ray is awaiting his companions for the Margate Pier trip to scatter Jack's ashes. As in Faulkner's *As I Lay Dying*, there is a grimly comic element to this gathering and the journey, a fact emphasized by the container for Jack's ashes, which instead of being a holy grail prosaically resembles an instant coffee jar; yet at its heart the 'pilgrimage' to Margate proves to be a deeply epiphanic experience for the four men involved. As already noted, *Last Orders* resembles *As I Lay Dying* in that it is structured around a series of monologues concerning themselves with events both past and present, but this structure also echoes the 'polyphonic' quality of Chaucer's poem with its inset stories and narratives (Phillips 2000: 2). Interestingly, Chaucer's own structure of a group of storytellers from diverse origins, 'sondry folk' (1986: General Prologue, l. 25), gathered together in a place and for a purpose has numerous literary counterparts, across the centuries and across cultures, from Boccaccio's fifteenth-century Florentine tale-tellers in the *Decameron*, brought together in a country house by an outbreak of plague, to Rana Dasgupta's global community stranded in an airport terminal by bad weather in his novel *Tokyo Cancelled* (2005).

Chaucer's pilgrims travelled on horseback; Faulkner's grotesque funeral procession moved forward by a combination of horse and wagon; Swift's protagonists travel in a royal blue Mercedes or 'Merc' provided by Vince, a used-car salesman. The car thus becomes in *Last Orders* an emblem of the new mobility of south Londoners; an ease of movement, social and geographical, that pulls figures like Vince away from the family trade of butchery, and renders trips to Kent simple and almost insignificant compared to the much-remembered and recounted hop-picking trips in the 1930s.

Last Orders, like *As I Lay Dying,* but also like the organized pilgrimages of the Middle Ages, is mapped out by means of various named specific places, way-stations, and markers, which carry meanings both for the past and present: 'The four men, compelled by a common errand, travel together across a small part of England, making discoveries about themselves, each other, their world, time, and history' (Cooper 2002: 23). Part of considering that historical process for Swift involves an engagement with England's past. One crucial cinematic intertext is Michael Powell and Emeric Pressburger's wartime rumination on English identity, *A Canterbury Tale* (1944), in which four poeple make a journey to Canterbury that is clearly suggestive of pilgrimage. Critics have also identified allusions to the Old English poems *Wanderer* and *Seafarer* (Cooper 2002: 32) in the novel's interest in different landscapes: land, *terra firma,* sea. Most obviously we have a version of land's end on Margate pier at the close, as well as desert and sea settings in the remembered war experiences of several of the men. Dee Dyas (2001: 23) has indicated how *Wanderer* and *Seafarer* themselves used biblical parallels, and Cooper has rightly traced elements of the Edenic storyline in *Last Orders* in the Cain and Abel struggle between Lenny and Vince. Swift's extended funeral procession both is and is not, then, a secular version of the medieval pilgrimage, just as Chaucer's pilgrims in *The Canterbury Tales* are a mix of the mercantilist, the self-serving, and the pious.

The four men in Swift's novel start their journey in April when there are 'daffs out on the verges' (30), and with a sense of promise, just as Chaucer's poem so famously begins. But this is also an elegiac poem in prose. The novel is a journey through post-imperial England; the narrative refrain reflects on how things have changed for the British male. For this journey is undoubtedly a male enterprise. The wife of this novel, Amy, is no travelling Wife of Bath; she chooses to stay behind, resisting the grim irony of going to Margate with Jack's ashes which was a journey she had planned to make with him in life, in their retirement. Amy's abiding sense of a journey in the novel is the far smaller, repetitive No. 44 bus route she makes to see hers and Jack's mentally impaired daughter in hospital.

In Swift's novel we are offered social topicality and topography as with Chaucer, but we also receive a version of the literary England that Chaucer's text forms a part of. The England of *Last Orders*, also invoked in that multiply referential title, is both changing and oddly timeless, on its last legs and yet enduring. And that in a way begins to unpack an answer to the charges of plagiarism levelled at this novel in relation to Faulkner's *As I Lay Dying*. Of course the Faulknerian intertext is crucial, revealing, moving even, in highlighting the South London analogue that Swift provides to the Mississippi regional literature of the 1930s. But, as Cooper has noted before me, we are not dealing with a single frame of appropriation or intertextuality but rather a 'symphony of intertexts'. It is in how these intertexts play off against each other that the full story of *Last Orders* emerges (2002: 37).

The musical metaphor of the symphony of texts or polyphony of voices in *Last Orders* is helpful, since it is one of the major contentions of this volume that in searching for ways of articulating the processes of adaptation and appropriation we need a more active vocabulary. A kinetic vocabulary, as I have termed it, is one that would be dynamic, moving forward rather than conducting the purely backward-looking search for source or origin. Swift's own favoured metaphor of the journey is certainly a useful point of reference: in studying the various interpretations and reinterpretations of canonical or established texts we are on a journey of sorts that takes us through various historical and geographical staging points. But there is also a danger in deploying the motif of the journey. As a term that seems to insist on a beginning and an end-point, an origin and a destination, the idea of a journey can reduce the adaptive process to a linear teleology. In truth, Swift's narrative technique is far more anti-linear than this implies: in its evocation of Old English and Middle English literature alone his narrative processes prove circular and intertwining rather than a direct movement from A to B (the circuitous narratives of Faulkner's *As I Lay Dying* perform a similar function).

The four men's journey to Margate also returns them to the past. Swift has deployed this anti-linear understanding of the textuality of history before, most notably in *Waterland*, and it is a psychic and narrative movement that informs his intertextual style. But it is perhaps in music and musicology that some of the most enabling metaphors for the kinetic process of adaptation might be sought. Much European baroque music in the sixteenth and seventeenth centuries derived its creational and performative impetus from improvising on dance music and patternings, working with such forms as the *bergamasca*, the *folia*, and the *passamezzo*. Improvisation or variation on a firm foundation or intertextual base is therefore fundamental to its composition and structure. Musical creations by Diego Ortiz, Marco Uccellini, and Henry Purcell, in Spain, Italy and England respectively, were commonly structured in terms of 'grounds' or repeated harmonic base instrumental patterns, often played by lute, harpsichord, or cello, or a combination of both, on the surface of which the more improvisational lines of instrumentation are performed by flute, recorder, bass viol, or violin. We have in this a rather beautiful model for the way in which intertext(s) in a novel such as *Last Orders* might operate as the base or 'ground' for the reader, informing the top note or improvisation that is the new creative act or cultural production. Eliot's notion of 'Tradition and the Individual Talent' seems to find new aesthetic life in this context.

Perhaps one of the best known musical contexts in which this ongoing, yet circular process of innovation upon a base 'ground' takes place is Johann Sebastian Bach's *Aria mit verscheidenen Veraenderungen* ('Aria with Different Variations'), better known as *The Goldberg Variations*. There are thirty variations framed by an opening and closing performance of the base aria. As Richard Powers so eloquently describes in his remarkable novel *The Gold Bug Variations* (discussed further in Chapter 9):

> The set is built around a scheme of infinitely supple, proliferating relations. Each of the thirty is a complete ontogeny, unfolding until it denies that it differs at its conception from all siblings by only the smallest mutation ... an imperceptibly vast *chaconne*, an evolutionary *passacaglia* built on the repetition and recycling of this Base.
>
> (1991: 578)

Powers's own metaphorical point of reference here is the genetic pat-terning revealed by research into DNA in the 1940s and 1950s, and the identification of the intertwined double helix by Crick and Watson. But what his prose gives us is an invaluable set of terms for rethinking the process of adaptation, moving away from a static or purely linear stand-point. Unfoldings, recyclings, mutations, repetitions, evolutions, varia-tions: the possibilities are endless and exciting.

A modern musical counterpart to baroque music's deployment of grounds can be found in the improvisational qualities of jazz. Jazz riffs, themselves models of repetition with variation, frequently make refer-ence or pay homage to base canonical works (see also McClary 2001). One potent example of this is Duke Ellington's suite *Such Sweet Thunder* based on several Shakespearean plays and sonnets (1999 [1957]). Ellington's virtuoso interpretations of the Shakespearean base texts per-fectly exemplifies Henry Louis Gates Jr's theory of 'signifying' in African-American culture, as invoked in the introduction, which Gates adopted from the practice and example of prominent jazz musicians: 'In the jazz tradition, compositions by Count Basie ("signify") and Oscar Peterson ("signifying") are structured around the ideas of formal revi-sion and implication' (1988: 123).

Even more recently we have the working example of sampling in musical genres such as rap and hip-hop. David Hesmondhalgh has provocatively described this as plagiarism as a cultural tactic or inter-ventionist act, indicating ways in which debates about plagiarism and intellectual and literary property rights need to be remobilized in more positive, socially productive, and empowering ways. Exploring what he describes as the 'tangled' sounds of rap, Hesmondhalgh queries the extent to which rap's interest in appropriation, intertextuality, and 'recontextualization' can be subjected to conventional copyright law: 'To what extent does the act of recontextualization, the placing of the sam-ple next to other sounds, mean that authorship (and the resultant finan-cial rewards) should be attributed to those sampling, rather than those sampled?' (2000: 280). As with the furore over Swift's *Last Orders* we are dealing with a complex ethics of indebtedness, although with the added complication pointed out by David Sanjek that musical language does not carry quotation marks (1994: 349). Perhaps as with some of these more celebratory recognitions of the potential of rap or sampling to fos-

ter a new aesthetic, we need to view literary adaptation and appropriation from this more positive vantage point, seeing it as creating new
cultural and aesthetic possibilities that stand alongside the texts which
have inspired them, enriching rather than 'robbing' them. This would
provide 'grounds' perhaps for exonerating Graham Swift, and establishing a more vibrant method of exploring the appropriative process.

PART 2

LITERARY ARCHETYPES

3

'HERE'S A STRANGE ALTERATION': SHAKESPEAREAN APPROPRIATIONS

Adaptation and appropriation are dependent on the literary canon for the provision of a shared body of storylines, themes, characters, and ideas upon which their creative variations can be made. The spectator or reader must be able to participate in the play of similarity and difference perceived between the original, source, or inspiration to appreciate fully the reshaping or rewriting undertaken by the adaptive text. There are particular bodies of texts and source material, such as myth, fairy tale, and folklore which by their very nature depend on a communality of understanding. These forms and genres have cross-cultural, often cross-historical, readerships; they are stories and tales which appear across the boundaries of cultural difference and which are handed on, albeit in transmuted and translated forms, through the generations. In this sense they participate in a very active way in a shared community of knowledge, and they have therefore proved particularly rich sources for adaptation and appropriation. The following two chapters will consider myth and fairy tale in greater detail, but before turning to them, it seems crucial for any historicized study of the adaptive process to touch base with the playwright whose *oeuvre* functions in a remarkably similar way to the communal, shared, transcultural, and transhistorical art forms of myth and fairy tale: William Shakespeare.

It is no coincidence that the Shakespearean canon has provided a crucial touchstone for the scholarship of appropriation as a literary practice and form. Several book-length studies have considered appropriation from a Shakespearean perspective (see, for example, Marsden 1991; Chedgzoy 1995; Novy 1999; Desmet and Sawyer 1999; Fischlin and Fortier 2000; Sanders 2001; Zabus 2002). To cite Daniel Fischlin and Mark Fortier in the valuable overview essay that accompanies their recent anthology of dramatic adaptations of Shakespearean plays: 'As long as there have been plays by Shakespeare, there have been adaptations of those plays' (2000: 1). Dramatic adaptation of Shakespearean playtexts had become routine as early as the Restoration in England; from 1660 onwards playwrights such as Nahum Tate and William Davenant changed plotlines, added characters, and set to music Shakespearean scripts for performance (Clark 1997). And it does not stop at plays: poetry, novels, films, animations, television advertisements, have all engaged with Shakespeare as both icon and author. As Fischlin and Fortier point out, the Latin etymological root of the word 'adapt', *adaptare*, means 'to make fit' (2000: 3). The adaptation of Shakespeare invariably makes him 'fit' for new cultural contexts and different political ideologies to those of his own age. As a result, a historiographical approach to Shakespearean appropriation becomes in many respects a study of theoretical movements; many theories which had their intellectual foundation in recent decades, such as feminism, postmodernism, structuralism, gay and lesbian studies or queer theory, and postcolonialism, have had a profound effect on the modes and methodologies of adapting Shakespeare.

The ongoing adaptation of central figures of Western culture such as Shakespeare raises all kinds of questions about originality, authorship, and intellectual property rights. Some authors are accused of seeking to authenticate their own work by attaching the Shakespearean aura and reputation to their writing. Such writers are assumed to have a celebratory or honorific approach to their source. Others are seen to be more iconoclastic in intention, rewriting or 'talking back' to Shakespeare as an embodiment of the conservative politics, imperialism, and patriarchalism of a previous age. Whatever the ideological stance(s) of his adaptors, one inescapable fact is that Shakespeare was himself an active adaptor and imitator, an appropriator of myth, fairy tale, and folklore, as well as of the works of specific writers as varied as Ovid, Plutarch, and Holinshed. The early twentieth century witnessed a veritable industry in Shakespearean source-spotting; Geoffrey Bullough's influential eight-volume series, *Narrative and Dramatic Sources of Shakespeare*, was, and still is, a standard presence in any university library. The organization of Bullough's volumes proves instructive (Fischlin and Fortier 2000: 9). He divides his chapters in accordance with the following categories: direct source, analogue, translation, possible source, and probable source. The direct sources include Cinthio's prose text on a jealous Moor, reworked as *Othello*, the story of 'Pyramus and Thisbe' from Ovid's *Metamorphoses*, which is performed by the mechanicals in *A Midsummer Night's Dream*'s play-within-a-play, and Thomas Lodge's *Rosalynd*, incorporated into *As You Like It*. In many of these instances whole plotlines are lifted, assimilated, and recontextualized by Shakespeare. Elsewhere sustained allusions and analogues figure, such as Prospero's delivery of a speech in *The Tempest* translated from Ovid and spoken in the *Metamorphoses* by the sorceress Medea (5.1.33–56). That Prospero speaks in this way links his magic to rather darker arts than might be presumed from his heroic stance, and twins him in fascinating ways with the unseen but constantly invoked witch of the play, Caliban's mother Sycorax. Any study of Shakespeare's adaptation of sources indicates the rich intertextual readings such incorporation makes possible, although in an effort to stress Shakespeare's creativity as well as dependency, critics have been anxious to identify those moments where the dramatist supplements or amplifies his sources. One fine example of this is his addition of the commentator figure of Enobarbus to the tragic love story of *Antony and Cleopatra* which he derived from Plutarch.

All of the diverse methods of adaptation that we have been exploring in this volume apply to Shakespeare's varied personal practice of appropriation. Recent critical studies of the early modern period have tried to stress the collaborative writing environment in which Shakespeare worked. For example, he co-authored plays such as *The Two Noble Kinsmen* and *Henry VIII, or All is True* with John Fletcher. Perhaps a useful way of beginning to think about adaptation is as a form of collaboration across time and sometimes across culture or language. Shakespeare's age had a far more open approach to literary borrowing and imitation than the modern era of copyright and property law encourages or even allows. Imitation was learned and practised in schools and continued into adult writing careers. Shakespeare would perhaps have expected to be adapted by future writers and future ages. Jean Marsden has suggested that Ben Jonson's famous observation that Shakespeare 'was not of an age but for all time' need not be taken to endorse the hoary old claims to his 'universality' but rather as an indication that he remain available to subsequent ages to adapt and adopt as they wish. His cultural value lies in his availability; as Marsden notes, 'each new generation attempts to redefine Shakespeare's genius in contemporary terms, projecting its desires and anxieties onto his work' (1991: 1).

Returning to issues of the canon already raised by efforts to define terms in this study, Shakespeare is so frequently adapted in part because he is a major author (Fischlin and Fortier 2000: 6). There are also economic and legal factors: Shakespeare is helpfully outside copyright law, making him safe as well as interesting to adapt. The response, though, is varied: 'adaptors of Shakespeare undertake a number of responses to Shakespeare's canonical status: some seek to supplant or overthrow; others borrow from Shakespeare's status to give resonance to their own efforts' (Fischlin and Fortier 2000: 6). Shakespeare is constantly being made new, remade, by this process: 'if adaptations of Shakespeare somehow reinforce Shakespeare's position in the canon ... it is a different Shakespeare that is at work' (Fischlin and Fortier 2000: 6). The dramatic form encourages persistent reworking and imagining. Performance is an inherently adaptive art; each staging is a collaborative interpretation, one which often reworks a playscript to acknowledge contemporary concerns or issues. In the twentieth century, for example, *Henry V* has been re-envisioned as a play about the Second World War, Vietnam, the Falklands crisis, and more recently the two Gulf wars.

If drama embodies within its generic conventions an invitation to reinterpretation, so the movement into a different generic mode can encourage a reading of the Shakespearean text from a new or revised point of view. Stage plays famously offer broader perspectives on scenes and events than the single point of view of a film camera or a first person narrator in a novel. Admittedly there will be moments in a play when the individual fills the frame, during soliloquy for example, but this is not usually sustained across a whole performance. A novel written from a specific point of view can therefore adopt a radical slant on a play simply by choosing to focus in on a single character and their reaction to events.

The transfocalization involved in seeing things from this different point of view is a driving force in many non-Shakespearean appropriations as well, as we will see in the third section of this volume, not least in novels such as Jean Rhys's *Wide Sargasso Sea* or Peter Carey's *Jack Maggs*. These narratives are voiced wholly or in part by marginalized characters from canonical fiction (Charlotte Brontë's *Jane Eyre* and Charles Dickens's *Great Expectations*). J. M. Coetzee's *Foe* re-envisions Daniel Defoe's *Robinson Crusoe* from a female perspective entirely absent from the original text. In each of these instances an informed knowledge of the hypotext, or source, is crucial to appreciate the twists and turns of the adaptive text: 'The hypertext invites us to engage in a relational reading' (Genette 1997 [1982]: 399). In the cited examples from Rhys and Coetzee those twists and turns are also achieved via the introduction of the specific perspective, and bias, of first person narrative. Christy Desmet and Robert Sawyer make the intriguing point, in respect of Shakespearean appropriation, that this interest in entering the text from the perspective of a particular character, and therefore from a new angle, can at times seems a very outmoded form of 'character criticism' (1999: 10). But there is also a wilful misreading of the 'parent text' implicit in these rewritings that suggests a more politicized stance on the part of the literary 'offspring' than mere character criticism would imply.

Novels and poems which have sought to reshape Shakespeare have certainly exhibited a strong interest in first person narrative or the poetic persona. Jane Smiley's *A Thousand Acres*, for example, not only relocates the family struggle for control of land and emotions in *King Lear* to the American mid-west of the 1980s, but chooses to view events from the perspective of Ginny, the eldest daughter of Larry Cook, the farmer-patriarch whose division of his land promotes the internal jealousies and ruptures in the family that promulgate the events of the novel. If Larry is an analogue for Lear, the king's madness mirrored here in an encroaching form of dementia, then Ginny stands for Goneril. By allowing Ginny a developed voice and personal history, one which eventually exposes incest at the heart of this close-knit family, Smiley is able to 'flesh out' Goneril's violent actions against her father in the play. It is an example of the process of revaluation outlined by Genette in *Palimpsests*: 'The revaluation of a character consists in investing him or her – by way of pragmatic or psychological transformation – with a more significant and/or more "attractive" role in the value system of the hypertext than was the case in the hypotext' (1997 [1982]: 343).

If in *King Lear* Goneril's limited stage time and lines reduce her actions to a tragicomic grotesque version of villainy, such as when she poisons her sister Regan in a fight for the sexual attentions of Edmund, Smiley accords Ginny considerable motivation, psychological and physical, for her actions. The poisoning plotline resurfaces in the novel but constitutes a failed attempt by Ginny to wreak revenge on her sister Rose (Regan) for a shared relationship with neighbour Jess Cook. The Cook family storyline provides the narrative's analogue to the subplot in *King Lear*, the rivalry between the Duke of Gloucester's two sons and Gloucester's eventual blinding. It is a mark of the detailed relocation of the events of the play that the blinding in *A Thousand Acres* occurs as a result of an agricultural accident rather than the vicious torture witnessed onstage in Shakespeare's drama. Smiley's motivations in this rewriting of *King Lear* are multiple. She clearly felt a need to 'write back' to Shakespeare's demonization of female characters such as Goneril and Regan, to consider what might have motivated or caused such behaviour, indulging in the retrieval of female experience from a male-authored master-narrative (Zabus 2002: 6). She also writes from a late twentieth-century ecofeminist standpoint in terms of the novel's supplementary political and ecological concerns with the pollution of the land by so-called conventional farming techniques and the materialistic aims of modern capitalism and business practice (Mathieson 1999: 127–44; Sanders 2001: 191–216).

Marina Warner's novel *Indigo, or Mapping the Waters* exhibits a similar interest in retrieving the woman's story from a male-centred text. This time the focus is Shakespeare's *The Tempest*. Warner's narrative, which will also be examined in Chapter 5 in terms of its appropriation of fairy tale, offers an extended voice to two of that play's marginalized female characters, Miranda and Sycorax. If Miranda is subject to her father's controlling presence throughout the play, Sycorax is reduced to the accounts provided by others; she is only talked of, never seen. Warner's novel, in a tactic familiar to several of the novel appropriations considered here, interweaves a double time-scheme to depict Miranda in the twentieth century and Sycorax in the early modern period. Warner resists, however, the simplistic linearity of historical account. *Indigo* challenges the stability of such accounts, subjecting history to the patterns of storytelling and multiple textualities (the theoretical underpinning of these ideas of the textuality of history or history as narrative are explored in more detail in Chapter 8 of this volume). This enables a feminist viewpoint to be articulated.

Framing the entire narrative is the storytelling of Serafine Killabree, a figure who connects both with Sycorax and Miranda, thereby drawing the novel into a more circular mode of being than the teleology of 'History' allows. In turn, a critical, postfeminist, and postcolonial reading of *The Tempest* is incorporated into this revisionist text (Chedgzoy 1995: 94–134). It is an example of what Steven Connor has called 'fidelity-in-betrayal', 'more of an improvisation upon its original than an attempt to translate it' (1996: 186):

> If rewriting of this kind compromises the cultural authority of the original text, then this never amounts to a simple denial of it; in its attention to its rewritten original, its fidelity-in-betrayal, the rewritten text must always submit to the authority of an imperative that is at once ethical and historical.
>
> (Connor 1996: 167)

No simple denial or rejection of Shakespeare's play is made in *Indigo*, since it is by no means as straightforward a 'rewriting' as this would require, but its tenets and themes are re-viewed through a postcolonial lens. As Warner's acknowledgements to scholars such as Peter Hulme in the foreword indicate, this novel is a further instance of appropriation informed by critical history.

Few of the approaches or techniques identified in this chapter are exclusive to Shakespearean appropriation, but it seems fair to claim that the Shakespearean canon has served as a test bed over many centuries for the processes of adaptation. The history of Shakespearean re-visions provides a cultural barometer for the practice and politics of adaptation and appropriation. Much of the reworking impulse has engaged with the figure, biography, and cultural commodity of Shakespeare himself. Cinematic and dramatic texts that adapt and adopt the figure of Shakespeare include John Madden's *Shakespeare in Love* (1998) and Edward Bond's play *Bingo* (1983). The engagements with the 'myth of

Shakespeare' these represent have been considered elsewhere (see, for example, Holderness 1988), but what is of particular interest here is the way in which specific Shakespearean plays have proved especially resonant for adaptors in the twentieth century, providing what James Andreas Sr calls 'aesthetic challenges' (1999: 107).

A statistical analysis of those texts by Shakespeare which are adapted most regularly, and again it is necessary to stress that we are thinking about prolonged engagement rather than passing allusion, would reveal three plays at the top of the list: *The Tempest*, *Othello,* and *Hamlet*. In the case of *The Tempest* and *Othello*, we need to look to the British colonial legacy and to Shakespeare's function within the multiculturalism of the twentieth-century literary enterprise for some answers. Shakespeare was undoubtedly deployed as a tool of empire, taught in schools across the world as a means of promoting the English language and the British imperial agenda. As a result, postcolonial texts that 'talk back' to the colonizing culture frequently deploy Shakespeare as a means of achieving this. There are complex reasons at stake: as products of imperial and imperialist educational structures, many of these writers share knowledge of Shakespeare with the dominant culture they seek to critique. If adaptation requires foreknowledge of the source for the system of analogue and juxtaposition to succeed, as we have argued elsewhere, then Shakespeare is a reliable cultural touchstone, a language 'we all understand'.

Certain texts, however, also carry a particular freightage of meaning where postcolonial politics are concerned. *The Tempest* became canonical in postcolonial studies in the late twentieth century, harnessed as it was in performance and revisionary writing to think about both the discovery of the 'New World' of the Americas and the British imperial project in Africa and elsewhere (Zabus 2002). *Othello* is a text that deals with racism within its dialogue and action and it has therefore also proved a rich source for texts seeking to examine the tensions of multicultural societies in the modern era. In a 2001 film appropriation of the play, '*O*', director Tim Blake Nelson relocated the storyline to a US college. Odin James (Othello) is a top flight basketball player on the college team, engaged in a passionate relationship with a fellow student Dessie. The envious Hugo is the team coach's son. In the hothouse atmosphere and competitive world of college sports, Blake Nelson finds a perfect analogue for the complicated military friendships and rivalries of the play.

It is no coincidence that Odin's initials, O. J., recall another African-American US sports star accused of murdering his white wife, O. J. Simpson. By exploring contemporary issues in the US via the filtering lens of the Shakespearean tragedy, Blake Nelson in turn exposes the class rivalries and racism implicit in the US education system. The film suffered a lengthy delay before its public release due to retrospective parallels found in its scenes of college shootings with the Columbine High School massacre of 1999.

The trial of O. J. Simpson is also recalled in another modern variation upon the *Othello* theme which offers an African-American perspective on the Shakespearean source. With each scene framed by audio recordings of significant black events and speeches, such as Martin Luther King's Washington address, Malcolm X, Louis Farakhan and the Million Man March, O. J. Simpson's trial, and the sexual harassment hearings involving Anita Hill and Supreme Court judge Clarence Thomas, Djanet Sears's *Harlem Duet* is a play with a triple interwoven time-scheme. Juxtaposed scenes depict Harlem in the 1850s and the 1860s, that is to say during the years leading up to the American Civil War, and in the 1920s, and the 1990s that were contemporary to the play's first production. Its events serve as a prequel to the events of Shakespeare's play in the sense that the modern Othello in this text is a Columbia University Literature professor who has left his partner for a white colleague, Mona. Audiences are being invited to 'read in' the future for these characters using the Shakespearean tragedy as a template. Mona is Desdemona, Chris Yago, the jealous colleague, is Iago, and the summer-school position Othello accepts in Cyprus bodes ill. The play is a complex rumination on the history of black representation in the theatre as well as a clever appropriation of *Othello*: it is telling, for example, that the white character of Mona is only seen by means of a disembodied voice and arm in performance. There are numerous inversions of the Shakespearean original as well as recognizable motifs and signifiers such as the handkerchief. For Fischlin and Fortier who include it in their anthology of Shakespearean adaptations, 'Shakespeare's text remains a barely visible (but nonetheless significant) backdrop ...' (2000: 287). Sears's production is evocatively devised around musical rhythms and signifiers. It has an aesthetic structure derived in part from blues and jazz music. The 'duet' of the title is performed not only by the various allusive partnerships in the play but by the instruments of cello and double bass. This musical frame serves to emphasize a black contribution to the arts in the Americas but also underscores Sears's own improvisational approach to the Shakespearean playtext. Henry Louis Gates Jr's notions of 'signifying' are again relevant (1988; Andreas Sr 1999: 107). *The Tempest* and *Othello* are traditional paradigms for any postcolonial scholar or writer; their presence operates as a musical refrain in itself, although one rewritten and reconceptualized at every turn.

Hamlet also has canonical standing in any study of Shakespearean reception and appropriation. This is not because of specifically postcolonial or feminist appropriations, although Ophelia's tragic trajectory has been of considerable interest to female adaptors, not least Angela Carter, whose novels and short stories are haunted by the image of Ophelia in her madness (Sage 1994: 33). What places *Hamlet* at the centre of the twentieth-century literary canon is the influence of Freud and theories of psychoanalysis. As the exploration of a mind in crisis, the play has proved attractive to many commentators, not least T. S. Eliot whose essays and interests in the earlier part of that century proved influential in the shaping of the discipline and concerns of English Literature.

One factor that has amplified or extended the canonicity of *Hamlet* is that the Prince of Denmark has come to be regarded as the culminating role for any aspiring young actor. It serves, then, as a career touchstone as well as a literary one. In a related vein, film adaptations of the play have burgeoned, ranging from Laurence Olivier's Freud-imbued 1948 black-and-white rendition, which carried the voiceover declaration that this was the tragedy 'of a man who cannot make up his mind' (Rothwell 1999: 59), through Franco Zeffirelli's Gothic rendition of the 1990s taste for the action movie to Kenneth Branagh's so-called 'full text' version in 1996. As mentioned in Chapter 1, in 2000 Michael Almereyda produced his *Hamlet*, set in a millennial Manhattan. The corporate values of the late twentieth century substituted for the early modern play's plotlines of dynastic rivalry and cross-border battles. The Castle of Elsinore was replaced by the Denmark Corporation, with Claudius as a manipulative CEO. In this version, both Hamlet and Ophelia were art students, enabling some suggestive (post)modern substitutions for the play's central moments: Ophelia's distribution of symbolic flowers in her madness was represented by the giving of photographic representations of the same; 'The Mousetrap', *Hamlet*'s play-within-a-play, became a film collage shot on 16 mm by Ethan Hawke's media studies 'prince'. Once again, the filtration effect of adaptations influencing further adaptations cannot be ignored. A chronological study of Shakespearean adaptation uncovers all manner of cross-fertilization; in this case, Almereyda's acknowledged influence in creating a corporate *mise-en-scène* for *Hamlet* is Akira Kurosawa's 1960 film *The Bad Sleep Well*, which relocated the play to the Tokyo Stock Exchange. Similar interactions can be explored between William Reilly's previously cited *Men of Respect* (1990) and Ken Hughes's *Joe Macbeth* (1955), both gangland ruminations on *Macbeth*, and Gus Van Sant's remarkable transposition of the Hal-Falstaff relationship of the *Henriad* in *My Own Private Idaho* (1991) and Orson Welles's film version of those plays, *Chimes at Midnight* (1966).

Film adaptation is one important sub-set of adaptation and appropriation that invariably signals its relationship to the Shakespearean play-text(s) in a straightforward manner, usually by means of the title. But there are further sub-groups which deploy a sourcetext as a creative springboard for another, often wholly different, text, a movement also signalled frequently by title. This creative move is sometimes achieved by extrapolating a particular storyline or character's trajectory from the original, and reimagining it in a new context, historical and/or cultural. The relationship to the original remains present and relevant, but it is as if a grafting has taken place of a segment, or rootstock, of the original text. The rootstock is conjoined to a new textual form, or scion, to create a wholly new literary artefact. I am deploying these metaphors of grafting quite self-consciously. Not only did Shakespeare deploy the metaphor in *The Winter's Tale* (4.4.87–97), but Gérard Genette uses this exact phrase to describe the adaptive relationship between hypotext (original) and hypertext (recreation) (1997 [1982]: ix). In this notion of rootstock and scion being brought together by the grafting process to create a new plant (pear trees, for example, are always grown on quince rooting stocks) literature has long found a rich source of metaphor for its own creative practices. Shakespeare's sonnets abound with the imagery of grafting and Eliot's notion of tradition and the individual talent finds an intriguing analogue in this horticultural practice.

Perhaps one of the most influential 'grafts' of Shakespearean drama is Tom Stoppard's 1967 play *Rosencrantz and Guildenstern are Dead*. This play melds an appropriative reading of Shakespeare's *Hamlet*, one which tries to imagine a back story for two minor characters who are Hamlet's former friends and attendant lords, with a quasi-parodic approach to the absurdist theatrical practices which were in the ascendant when Stoppard created his play. The other clear intertext for *Rosencrantz and Guildenstern are Dead* is Samuel Beckett's 1952 play *Waiting for Godot*. Stoppard creates his attendant lords in the image of Beckett's endlessly philosophizing tramps, Vladimir and Estragon, who for the majority of their play wait on a largely bare stage for something to happen. The opening stage direction makes this connection clear: '*Two Elizabethans passing the time in a place without any visible character*' (Stoppard 1990 [1967]: 9). The joke is that the audience, unlike Rosencrantz and Guildenstern, knows what will happen, because they know the script and therefore the outcome of *Hamlet*. Hence Rosencrantz and Guildenstern are already dead, even before they have started their play; we know only too well the plotline of the sea journey and the exchanged letters and their disappearance from the stage of Shakespeare's drama. The playtext exploits the idea of 'every exit being an entrance some-where else' (22); we see Rosencrantz and Guildenstern in their 'down-time' or offstage moments, the irony being that their *Hamlet* offstage is this play's onstage. Stoppard does not simply impose his themes on a Shakespearean framework. In many instances he finds precedent for his dramaturgical decisions in the Shakespearean precursor. For example, Elizabethan and Jacobean plays often began with attendant lords in dis-cussion (see, for example, *Antony and Cleopatra* or *King Lear*), and *Hamlet*, like *Rosencrantz and Guildenstern are Dead*, is interested in themes of broken ceremony, 'maimèd rites' (Shakespeare 1998: 5.1.214), and metatheatricality (Sale 1978: 83).

Stoppard's play is, however, hugely influential in that it chooses to re-view Hamlet from the theatrical sidelines, from the margins, and through the eyes of minor characters. This serves to render *Hamlet*, and in particular the figure of the prince, absurd. Aspects, events, and char-acters from Shakespeare's play are visible onstage during the course of Stoppard's drama, but these have often been creatively decentred, reduced to dumbshow or nonsensical fragment. The play's 'hero' is reduced to a slightly risible and histrionic character as a result. Many critics have described this as an exercise in postmodernism, fragmenting, defamiliarizing, and displacing as it does one of the most canonical texts of English literature and Western culture; Roger Sale also regards it as an act of depoliticization (1978: 83).

Seeing things from marginal, or even offstage, characters' points of view is a common drive in many adaptations and appropriations. When the dramatic genre is reworked into prose fiction form an intriguing equivalent is found for dramatic soliloquy in the form of first person narration. Postmodernist fiction with its investment in highlighting the modes of unreliable narration draws attention to the bias implicit in this vantage point, but what this biased perspective also allows in the rewriting of Shakespearean drama is the ability to see things from a particular character's point of view. Novelists are invariably drawn to the idea of seeing things from the perspective of a character who is marginalized or disenfranchised by the original play, be this for reasons of social status, gender or race. An ideological purpose to the revised perspective is almost inevitable as a result, and, as already argued, many Shakespearean appropriations are motivated not only by the desire to ascribe motivation, as exemplified in the (unreliable) first person narration of Smiley's *A Thousand Acres*, but also by political commitment. The theoretical concerns of postcolonialism, feminism, and queer theory, or a vibrant fusion of all these, figure in many adaptations of Shakespeare.

Contemporary American novelist John Updike indicates in an afterword to *Gertrude and Claudius* (2000) that a renewed awareness of 'offstage characters' in *Hamlet* derived from seeing Branagh's 1996 film version of the play was the spur to creating his novel. He does not choose to write from a first person perspective but his text is sympathetic to the situation of Hamlet's mother, Gertrude, who marries the brother-in-law who murdered her husband. Updike achieves this sympathetic approach by means of the timeframe which functions for the first two sections of his novel as a prequel to Shakespeare's play. We see how the young Gertrude, or Gerutha as she is called in Part 1 of the novel, a point to which we will return, was subject to the dynastic ambitions of her father when choosing a husband: 'And I am to be the plunder in exchange' (Updike 2000: 5). Her husband, Horwendil the Jute, proves a committed warrior but a rough lover. In this way, Updike imputes a motive to Gertrude's adultery which is not present in the Shakespearean precursor. This ascription of motive in turn manipulates or encourages the reader to respond with sympathy and understanding to Gertrude's predicament when she is seduced by the tender attentions of Horwendil's brother, Feng.

The variant and variable nomenclature of Updike's novel makes several important points in its own right. The novel has a tripartite structure, and although the events portrayed in each section are continuous in chronological terms, the main players' names alter in each section. The protagonists' names in Part 1 derive from the ancient *Hamlet* legend as detailed in Saxo Grammaticus's *Historia Danica* (1514): Gerutha, Horwendil the Jute, Feng his brother, Corambus, and Amleth. In Part 2 they derive from François de Belleforest's *Histoires tragiques* (Paris, 1576): Geruthe, Horvendile, Fengon, Corambis, and Hamblet. It is not until the third and final part that we get the more familiar Shakespearean nomenclature: Gertrude, King Hamlet, Claudius, Polonius, Hamlet. Updike adds a further textual layer in that Polonius is called Corambis in the quarto edition of Shakespeare's plays. This slippage between the names is an indication that *Hamlet* has many textual origins and provenances and that Shakespeare's play comes quite late in the line of adaptation and interpretation. That Shakespeare's drama is a variation on a much older theme is emphasized by Updike's decision to open each section with the same sentence: 'The King was irate.' Like Bach's *Goldberg Variations*, as discussed in Chapter 2, we are given the central aria (or in this instance plotline) on which many adaptors have ruminated and offered their own textual variants.

Any fixed or stable reading of the canonical Shakespearean playtext is effectively challenged by Updike; the rich textual provenance justifies his speculation with regard to motivation for the events of the play. Part 2 of *Gertrude and Claudius* ends with a brother's murder of a brother while he sleeps in an orchard, an event recalled in flashback by the Ghost in *Hamlet* (1.5.59–79). In Part 3, events as well as names offer more familiar signification to readers; we get direct quotation from the playtext, as well as recognizable events, not least the court celebrations for Gertrude and Claudius's 'o'er-hasty' marriage and Hamlet's 'muttered puns' (208) in response to his uncle's elaborate performance of duty of care in front of the Elsinore courtiers. But, as the alert reader will register, this is only the first act of *Hamlet* that we are seeing in the final part of this novel: much lies ahead. The tragic impetus is what feeds the reader's imagination and expectation in contradistinction to Claudius's: 'The era of Claudius had dawned; it would shine in Denmark's annals. He might, with moderation of his carousals, last another decade on the throne. Hamlet would be the perfect age of forty when the crown descended. He and Ophelia would have the royal heirs lined up like ducklings ... He had gotten away with it. All would be well' (210). The last phrase is an allusion to Claudius's prayer scene at 3.4 of *Hamlet* ('All may be well', 3.4.72), although the alert reader will note the shift from the subjunctive mode to one of (misplaced) certainty. The further juxtaposition of the Shakespearean frame of reference with contemporary US idiom ('gotten away with it') points up the playfulness of Updike's approach to his multiple sources.

The film adaptations of *Hamlet* and the appropriations of Stoppard and Updike discussed here have an explicit relationship to their Shakespearean precursor, but appropriation, as we saw in Chapter 2, need not always signal its intertextual relations in this explicit way. Appropriations can represent or suggest a range of relations ranging from 'direct contact to indirect absorption' (Miola 1992: 7). There are, therefore, those appropriations which derive a certain amount of comic or parodic impetus from their relationship with *Hamlet*. A useful working example of the latter would be Charlotte Jones's *Humble Boy* (2001). This is a play about a Cambridge astrophysicist, Felix Humble, who is traumatized by the death of his father, and troubled by his mother's relationship with another man. Felix's late father's hobby of bee-keeping enables lots of puns on those central lines from *Hamlet*, 'To be or not to be' and 'Let be'; the latter words form the closing line of Jones's play. There are also appropriations where the playtext features as what Robert Miola has usefully termed a 'deep source' (Miola 1992: 7); Graham Swift's *Ever After* and Alan Isler's *The Prince of West End Avenue* both appear to fit this category.

Swift's novel has a deeply introspective first person narrator, who is both haunted by the suicides of his (supposed) father and wife, and who has suicidal thoughts of his own; this in itself offers a parallel with Shakespeare's introspective protagonist: 'for a large part of my life ... I have imagined myself — surreptitiously, presumptuously, appropriately, perversely — as Hamlet. And you all know one of his tendencies' (Swift 1992: 4). The narrative style offers a further analogue to Hamlet's multiple self-analytical soliloquies in the play as well as pointing up the thin line between fact and invention. The narrator, Bill Unwin, whose name we only learn halfway through the novel, an indication of the extent to which his life and personality are determined by those around him, is an academic researcher. Despite his crippling self-doubt, compounded by the fact that his research fellowship is dependent upon the patronage of his step-father, Unwin is researching a set of family notebooks dating from the 1850s. These manuscripts record the crisis in faith experienced by his ancestor Matthew Pearce, who in the wake of evolutionary theory and the doubts it cast on a religious understanding of the world, sacrificed his marriage and family life to this growing state of 'unbelief'. In Chapter 7, we will investigate a series of novels that find their source material in the 1850s and 1860s and what might be termed the 'Darwinian' moment. Charles Darwin published *The Origin of Species* in 1859. Darwin's text is directly cited in *Ever After*. In working with this material as well as Shakespearean intertexts – as well as *Hamlet*, the narrative of *Ever After* alludes to *Love's Labour's Lost* and *Antony and Cleopatra* at crucial moments – Swift is paying homage to late twentieth-century fiction's interest in the impact of Darwin. One particular focus of Swift's intertextuality is John Fowles's postmodern recreation of the Victorian novel, *The French Lieutenant's Woman*, which, like *Ever After*, featured an 1850s geologist working in Lyme Regis (Fowles's novel is discussed in Chapter 7). Swift, as discussed in Chapter 2, is a writer deeply aware of his literary foundations and one whose narratives are steeped in a subtle and pervasive form of allusion and adaptation. He seems to encourage this account of his narrative technique via Bill Unwin's analysis of academic research as a complicated blend of fact and hypothesis, and the supplementation of the available material: 'Let's read between the lines' (211). Appropriation is frequently involved in a process of reading between the lines, offering analogues or supplements to what is available in a source text, and drawing attention to its gaps and absences. Swift's title is one that we inevitably supplement with an additional absent word and concept: happy (ever after).

Gaps in the narrative also help to define the complex textual operations of Alan Isler's *The Prince of West End Avenue*, a novel which ironically acknowledges its indebtedness to *Hamlet* in that deliberately bathetic or disjunctive title. It is set in a New York Jewish nursing home and narrated by another of our by-now-familiar unreliable first person narrators, Otto Korner. The narrative is couched as a memoir or confessional, although in a manner somewhat akin to Unwin's circuitous narrative in *Ever After* many of the revelations are withheld until near the very end. Despite his claim, 'I want to set the historical record straight' (Isler 1996: 2), Korner's narrative is full of suppression and evasion. Like Unwin (and Hamlet), he is haunted by ghosts from the past, not least memories of the Holocaust, but there is both a horror and an egotism in his seeming determination to place himself at the centre of twentieth-century historical events. We learn that he met Lenin and Joyce, that he is the forgotten founder, albeit by accident, of the Dada movement, and he even takes upon himself responsibility for Jewish deaths in the Nazi internment camps. This is because he failed to see the gravity of the situation in the 1930s and therefore persuaded his family to remain in Berlin. Undoubtedly their refusal to leave led to their internment and the subsequent deaths of Korner's wife and child, and the later suicide of his sister Lola; but the reader questions to what extent he can take on responsibility for all German Jews who chose to remain in their homeland in the face of emergent fascism.

The reader's response to Korner is a strange blend of sympathy and yet awareness of his deep egotism. That egotism, the desire to place himself at the centre of things, is comprehensible largely through the novel's intertextual relationship with *Hamlet*. In one of the novel's ironic gestures, the octogenarians in the residential home are staging their own version of *Hamlet*, a play-within-the-novel as it were. This encourages a whole series of comic comparisons and oddly dissonant juxtapositions: elderly Ophelias, for example, and, not least, several ironic linguistic echoes. In one instance, Hamlet's 'sea of troubles' from the 'To be or not to be' soliloquy (3.1.58–90 [61]) is reduced to Otto's constipation, a further example of the bathos central to this novel's technique: 'My troubles, it seems, may be solved by a valium, a muscle relaxant, and, inevitably, stewed fruit' (216). Yet for all the comic irony, there is a deeply serious subtext to this Jewish appropriation of *Hamlet*, one where the ghosts of public history are all too chilling and real.

Our questioning, as readers, of Otto's insistence on placing himself at the centre of this public history is in part negotiated by his attitude to, and our understanding of, Shakespeare's tragedy. Otto wants to play Hamlet in the nursing home's production: 'in the Prince of Denmark I see much of myself' (44). Initially, he is, to his chagrin, cast as the

Ghost, fitting perhaps for someone so haunted by his own remembrances. Then, due to the deaths of other cast members, he is 'promoted' to First Gravedigger. His response is to make the gravedigger's role equal to that of the prince: '*the Gravemaker and the Prince are the two faces of a single coin*' (98); 'May we not say, therefore, that it is the Gravemaker who leads Hamlet to his identity?' (99).

Korner's reading of *Hamlet* and understanding of his own position in history and society, real or otherwise, has a further intertextual referent, one which he directly cites: 'As Prufrock puts it, "I am not Prince Hamlet, nor was meant to be"' (22). The allusion is to T. S. Eliot's poem 'The Love Song of J. Alfred Prufrock', in which the ageing speaker of Eliot's dramatic monologue considers his own marginal role on the social stage by means of a comparison with the *dramatis personae* in *Hamlet* and other Shakespearean drama: 'No! I am not Prince Hamlet, nor was meant to be; / Am an attendant lord ...' (1969: 16). On the surface, as with Korner's declaration, there is a resignation here to a marginal role. And yet the reader who is in full command of Eliot's poem and Shakespearean drama can read on and reach a very different outcome about Prufrock's surface humility. For the role he eventually assigns himself ('Almost, at times, the Fool') could be seen, from a Shakespearean perspective, as pivotal. Eliot's choice of the upper case initial 'F' is crucial; Prufrock assigns himself the role of wise commentator. What a reading of *The Prince of West End Avenue* as an appropriation of *Hamlet* releases, then, is not only the comic-ironic material in the narrative, achieved as stated by a process of bathos and puncturing juxtapositions, but new depths to the twists and complexities of Korner's narration and self-perception.

Studies of Shakespearean adaptation and appropriation become a complex means of measuring and recording multiple acts of mediation and filtration. As with the body of postcolonial texts responding to *The Tempest* and *Othello*, appropriations are often as much in dialogue with other adaptations as with the Shakespearean sourcetext. This, perhaps, is the essence of literary archetypes: their availability for rewriting means that they are texts constantly in flux, constantly metamorphosing in the process of adaptation and retelling. They persistently enact and re-enact the activity of storytelling, and Shakespeare has provided some of the most familiar stories of Western culture. This is also the case with the two literary forms considered over the next two chapters: myth and fairy tale.

4

'IT'S A VERY OLD STORY': MYTH AND METAMORPHOSIS

A culture's mythology is its body of traditional narratives. Mythical literature depends upon, incites even, perpetual acts of reinterpretation in new contexts, a process that embodies the very idea of appropriation. In the introduction to this volume, Joyce's exploitation of mythic structures in *Ulysses* to evoke age-old, even universal, themes alongside time- and place-specific issues of politics and language was examined. Myth it seems lends itself to this dual plane of exploitation. As Roland Barthes asserts in *Mythologies*, 'the fundamental character of the mythical concept is to be appropriated' (1993 [1972]: 119). Barthes views this process in terms of a metalanguage communicated across generations and cultures, 'Mythical speech is made of a material which has *already* been worked on so as to make it suitable for communication ...' (110), but which is persistently relocated in a new social and cultural geography at each occasion of adaptation and appropriation. He invokes the specific example of a tree. Mentioned in a text, this undoubtedly stands for a tree in the literary context, a cross-cultural and cross-historical object, but it also becomes loaded with localized and particularized meaning according to its 'social geography' as Barthes call it; the tree is 'adapted to a certain type of consumption' (109), as, indeed, are myths. This form of adaptation, relocation, and recontextualization proves an expansive rather than reductive mode for Barthes; he argues that myths 'ripen' as they spread (149). Genette articulates the related concept of amplification, deploying the specific example of classical drama (1997 [1983]: 262). Tragic drama, he stresses, had its origins in the reworking of a few staple myths.

Each new generation of story-makers adopted familiar mythic templates and outlines for their storytelling purposes. Even writers, such as Ovid, Aeschylus, and Euripides, who we might consider to be the source of much contemporary literary and cinematic appropriation of myth, were themselves refashioning previous mythical traditions. But a myth is never transported wholesale into its new context; it undergoes its own metamorphoses in the process. Myth is continuously evoked, altered, and reworked, across cultures, and across generations. To cite Barthes again: 'there is no fixity in mythical concepts: they can come into being, alter, disintegrate, disappear completely' (120). All of these descriptions and critical formulations gesture at the metamorphic and transformative process of adaptation: the term functions literally as well as metaphorically. It is perhaps therefore no surprise that Ovid, the prime author of narratives of metamorphosis and transformation, has proved a particularly rich source for contemporary novelists, poets, playwrights and directors. As this chapter will demonstrate, his complex, generically hybrid texts, such as the *Metamorphoses* and the *Heroides*, which self-consciously blend the comic and tragic, appeal to the experimental and metafictional aspects of much modern and postmodern writing. As examples from authors such as Salman Rushdie and Kate Atkinson will indicate, Ovid's stories of metamorphosis offer a template for the artistic, and ideological, act of adaptation and re-vision; furthermore, specific stories from the Ovidian *oeuvre*, such as that of the poet-musician Orpheus and his doomed lover Eurydice, will prove to have offered a potent repository for re-visionary artists, attracting as diverse a community as the director Baz Luhrmann and the novelist Graham Swift.

MODERN METAMORPHOSES

Postmodern writing, we are constantly reminded, is a form in which the reader is asked to be aware of the constructing author, of the artifice of the piece. There is nothing new in this, as any reading of Ovid indicates. In the *Metamorphoses* Ovid persistently draws attention to the role of the storyteller: many of his best known accounts of metamorphosis and transformation, such as Pygmalion, Venus and Adonis, Leda and the Swan, and Danae and the golden shower, are inset narratives, contained within the storytelling, singing, or web-weaving of Orpheus, Arachne, and others. What mythical appropriations facilitate therefore is a means for contemporary authors to carry out self-conscious investigations into the artistic process. But Ovid's tales of shape-shifting and change, narratives that frequently occur under the pressure of particular events such as attempted rape or extreme grief, also find resonant parallels in many of the themes and concerns of those same writers. Myth extracts events from an everyday context into the world of gods and the supernatural, the extraordinary in the fullest sense of that term, and for this reason it has proved an especially attractive source for magic realist writers, such as Rushdie and Gabriel García Márquez, who seek to lift the quotidian event into a space of greater possibility. Magic realism or mythical appropriation is not a denial of real social issues: Alison Sharrock suggests that, despite its themes of gods and goddesses and worlds other than our own, myth 'allows space ... for the examination of family matters ...' (Hardie 2002: 105). As well as enabling the flights of fantasy associated with magic realism, then, myth is deployed to discuss the most familiar of subjects: families; love; fathers and daughters.

This potent blend of the extraordinary and the everyday has proved part of the appeal for a cluster of Ovidian appropriations in recent decades. Poets, including Seamus Heaney, Simon Armitage, Carol Ann Duffy, and Ted Hughes (who went on to write his full length *Tales from Ovid* in 1997), contributed work to the anthology *After Ovid* in 1994; prose writers ranging from A. S. Byatt and Joyce Carol Oates to the Dutch writer Cees Nooteboom wrote short stories for *Ovid Metamorphosed* in 2000. Many of these texts bring the mythical frame of reference quite literally down to earth. Oates's retelling of the death of Actaeon in 'The Sons of Angus MacElster', for example, recounts the demise of a violent Cape Breton patriarch; in her version the hunting hounds that tear Actaeon to pieces in the shape of a stag are MacElster's sons hacking at their father's drunken body in the barn after he has assaulted their mother (Terry 2000: 72–7). Carol Ann Duffy's 'Mrs. Midas' is a contemporary housewife, distraught to see the objects in her household rapidly turning to gold (Hofman and Lasdun 1994: 262).

The double drive apparent in the mythical appropriation process, which is a simultaneous invocation of the wondrous and the quotidian, is nowhere more evident than in the writings of Kate Atkinson. Atkinson's 1997 novel *Human Croquet*, a deeply intertextual creation that has been discussed elsewhere in terms of its Shakespearean allusions (Sanders 2001: 66–83), weaves its complex web of material, ranging from science fiction to the writings for young people of E. Nesbit and Enid Blyton, within a self-consciously Ovidian frame. As with the *Metamorphoses*, *Human Croquet* opens at the point of creation from chaos. Within its pages the specific tales of Daphne being turned into a laurel to escape Apollo's unwanted sexual attentions and of Phaeton's sisters transformed into trees by their excessive grief are alluded to. The novel's first person narrator, the excitable adolescent Isobel Fairfax, is studying Ovid and Shakespeare at school, so it does not surprise us that these writers form the shaping frames of reference for her thoughts. But Isobel is also overwhelmed by grief, like Hamlet or Phaeton's sisters. Their mother's violent death haunts Isobel and her brother Charles, who, in a grim reworking of fairy-tale, discovered her corpse in the woods: 'Absence of Eliza has shaped our lives' (Atkinson 1997: 28).

When Isobel is set the task by a schoolteacher of translating the passage on Phaeton's sisters from Ovid, she produces a highly emotional version of this tale of excessive, uncontainable grief (163). It is equally apposite that at various points in the narrative Isobel imagines her brother is metamorphosing into a dog: the Ovidian parallel is the story of Hecuba, another template of extreme grief, which in turn informed the lines of *Hamlet*. Hecuba was transformed into a canine state by her visceral mourning for her murdered husband King Priam:

> His ill-starred wife
> Lost, after all besides, her human shape;
> Her weird new barking terrified the breeze ...

> (Ovid 1987: 306)

Atkinson returns to Ovid in her recent collection of short stories, *Not the End of the World* (2002). Here, we encounter metamorphoses and transformations of various kinds, all based in recognizable modern contexts, a fact emphasized by Atkinson's easy allusions to brand names and popular television programmes. We meet, for example, Eddie, the product of a transgressive sexual liaison between his mother and Neptune on one memorable Cretan summer holiday; her story recalls those of Pasiphae and the bull, Leda and the swan, and numerous other tales of Jovean transformation into the shape of fish and fowl in order to seduce women that are recounted in the *Metamorphoses*. Enhancing our notion of Atkinson herself as a kind of Arachne, weaving her web of tales together, each of the stories finds resonance and echo in each other: characters recur, family connections are uncovered, and in one story a car crash is witnessed by a passer-by who in the previous tale had revealed to us a gruesome encounter with death in the shape of Hades on the M9 motorway. The entire collection is framed by the tragicomic story of Charlene and Trudi who find the reliable luxuries of modern life and shopping malls dessicating before their eyes following what appears to be a nuclear attack.

Atkinson's stories, as the collection's title both indicates and teasingly denies via the deployment of cliché, provide an apocalyptic image of millennial British society. Another writer who has deployed Ovid to a quasi-apocalyptic end is Salman Rushdie in his controversial novel, *The Satanic Verses* (1988). For Rushdie, however, metamorphosis becomes the means not just of imagining fantastical transformation, although his novel features many such examples, but the specific condition of the late twentieth-century migrant. The epigraph to his novel, taken from Daniel Defoe's *The History of the Devil*, provides a clue. It describes Satan as a vagabond, recalling in turn the wandering exile of John Milton's *Paradise Lost*, but the parallel with the modern migrant becomes clearest in the description of the devil as a person of 'unsettled condition … without any certain abode'. In the implicitly conservative value assigned by the Defoe quotation to being 'placed', to being of a fixed abode and society, Rushdie identifies a partial cause of the misplaced fear of immigrant communities. Rushdie's magic realism is central to his appropriation of Ovid, and specifically the text of the *Metamorphoses*. He invokes Ovid to create a fantastic world of hybrid shapes and mythical creatures, but then uses those creations to discuss social reality.

We start the novel with a 'fall'. That phrase has resonance in a Christian religious context, evoking the descent of the bad angels from heaven to hell (*Paradise Lost* is an intertext once again) as well as Eve's temptation of Adam with the apple of sexual knowledge. Rushdie is not afraid to play with these ideas of the fall as both a downfall and a creative act, or birth of sorts. In this sense, the fall is symbolic and yet the novel's opening is the literal, albeit fantastical, fall of two Bollywood actors from an Air India plane that has been exploded by hijackers. Describing this, Rushdie evokes mythic parallels by referring to the fall of Icarus: 'Just two brown men, falling hard, nothing so new about that, you may think; climbed too high, got above themselves, flew too close to the sun, is that it?' (Rushdie 1998 [1988]: 5). Significantly our protagonists are actors: their trade is one of representation in a novel that suggests modern life has become a simulacrum of reality. The influence of Jean Baudrillard's theories on Rushdie's writing cannot be underestimated. In *Simulacra and Simulation*, Baudrillard suggested that it was the postmodern condition that artificial, constructed worlds such as Disneyland or the cinema would come to appear more 'real' than reality (1981).

That Rushdie's actors originate from Bombay and 'Bollywood' film-making emphasizes this hyperreal Baudrillardian world of simulacra and representation. Bollywood has fashioned a reputation based on the appropriation of mythic templates and stock story-lines to great acclaim; even its nickname is an allusion to the supposed US precursor of Hollywood, and Rushdie finds humour in this – 'Bombay was a culture of re-makes. Its architecture mimicked the skyscraper, its cinema endlessly re-invented *The Magnificent Seven* ...' (64). But he is equally troubled by the implication that all Indian artistic creations have a Western 'original' or source. This corresponds to the concern in much postcolonial writing about the need to challenge or oppose these supposed 'originating sources', as we saw in the discussion of 'signifying' in the work of Henry Louis Gates Jr earlier. In the Rushdie quotation, the joke is on any reader who fails to notice that *The Magnificent Seven* is itself an intercultural cinematic appropriation of a Japanese 'original': Akira Kurosawa's *The Seven Samurai*.

As Gibreel and Saladin fall through what Rushdie describes as the ultimate twentieth-century site of 'air-space' (5), what they witness is Ovidian in the extreme: 'pushing their way out of the white came a succession of cloud forms, ceaselessly metamorphosing, gods into bulls, women into spiders, men into wolves' (6). The men land in 1980s

London, a place that both is and is not London, because it so tangibly fails to live up to any of their expectations. In *The Satanic Verses*, London and Bombay provide parallel, metamorphic, unstable cities. For Saladin Chamcha, formerly Salahuddin Chamchawala, whose father was significantly called Changez Chamchawala, and who was schooled in England, the pain of disappointed expectation is particularly deep. To assimilate into English society, Saladin attempts to alter his personality and appearance, only succeeding in estrangement from his Indian family and background. In the face of this failed metamorphosis, his body seems unable to halt the process of change. This results in the comic grotesque episode in the 'Black Maria' or police van, when Saladin, now in the shape of a satyr – half-man, half-goat – is arrested and brutally beaten by British police officers. What Rushdie finds in this Ovidian image is a means of suggesting the reduction of men like Chamcha into beasts by the prejudiced minds of the white police officers and others who engaged in racial attacks in 1980s Britain.

Rushdie captures in his mythical appropriation the dehumanized behaviour of those who perpetrate racial violence. Ovid's world of hybrid beasts, such as minotaurs, satyrs, and centaurs, is evoked not as an abstract 'world elsewhere' but as a means of addressing the brutalities and injustices of contemporary England. Only in the magical nighttime escape from the hospital of Saladin and hundreds of fellow beasts, who represent similarly brutalized asylum seekers and detainees, does Rushdie allow himself and the reader a moment of fantastic optimism. This is a memorable example of the amplification and ripening of myth argued for by Genette and Barthes. The Ovidian myth of metamorphosis is not lost in the process of adaptation into Atkinson's magic realist exploration of grief or in Rushdie's painful examination of the fate of the refugee, but much is added or gained.

The metalanguage of myth is deployed in these examples as an accessible code to discuss and communicate complex, and often troubling, ideas. Its additional deployment for political purposes, particularly in Rushdie, should also be registered. In turn, the persistently adaptable and malleable myth is given a newly relevant social and cultural geography. Metamorphosis would seem a particularly apposite concept to appropriate in this respect, but other Ovidian narratives have offered comparable potential for reworking, in particular that of Orpheus, the artist whose song continues beyond his narrative ending, beyond death. To an era interested in self-conscious accounts of the artistic process, his story has proved one of special interest and specific value.

ORPHIC NARRATIVES

Once and for all, it's Orpheus whenever there is song
Rainer Maria Rilke *Sonette an Orpheus* (1928)

Orpheus, a musician of great skill, marries the beautiful nymph Eurydice but she is killed by a fatal snakebite on their wedding day. Stricken with grief, Orpheus descends into the underworld to beg his wife's return to the living. Because his music proves so moving, he is granted his wish, but only on condition that when leading Eurydice out of the underworld, he does not once look back. Whether through love, fear or anxiety, Orpheus breaks this condition and Eurydice dies a second time. Barred from further re-entry into the underworld, Orpheus retires to woodland, mad with grief, shunning the company of women. A group of jealous females dismember him in a moment of pure Bacchic frenzy. In some versions of the tale Orpheus's decapitated head continues to sing until he is eventually reunited with Eurydice in the underworld. Ovid was not the first to relate the story of Orpheus in this form; Virgil had included it in Book 4 of the *Georgics*. Nevertheless, the significance of its placement in the narrative of the *Metamorphoses* has meant that Orpheus's story is inextricably linked with Ovid's work. The narrative of Orpheus and Eurydice occurs in Book 10 and his death is recounted in Book 11. Perhaps most significantly, Ovid's Orpheus is both a subject and a teller of stories. When he retires to the wilderness, he finds solace in singing tales which are warnings to resist 'destructive passion' (Bate 1993: 54). These tales include those of Ganymede, Hyacinth, Pygmalion, Myrrha, Venus and Adonis, and Atalanta. Orpheus's function as an embedded storyteller within the Ovidian narrative in part explains his availability to adapters and appropriators of subsequent centuries and generations. He is a prototype of the artist, be it musician, storyteller, painter or poet. This aspect of his story propels allusions to him in the work of Milton, Shelley, and Browning, among others (see Miles 1999: 61–195).

What we are dealing with in much mythic appropriation is an interest in archetypes. If Orpheus is viewed as the prototype of the artist, so his relationship with Eurydice is deployed as literary shorthand for extreme and enduring love. As with Romeo and Juliet, Orpheus and Eurydice have become archetypes of passionate love, their story reappearing in diverse cultural contexts from opera to contemporary film, from Brazil to South London. This availability for reworking gestures at the dual potential in myth identified both by Barthes's transcultural notion of a metalanguage but also by his articulation of the potential for culturally-specific contexts for the consumption of myth. The process of universalization remains, then, for Barthes a deeply political and politicized activity (1993 [1972]:142–5). Myth as archetype undoubtedly concerns itself with themes that endure across cultural and historical boundaries: love, death, family, revenge. These themes might in some contexts be deemed 'universal', and yet the essence of adaptation and appropriation renders the mythical archetype specific, localized, and particular to the moment of the creation.

The 1950s Brazilian film *Orfeu Negro* or *Black Orpheus* (dir. Marcel Camus, 1959), retains character names and the essential plotline of Orpheus and Eurydice's doomed passion but chooses to relocate the Ovidian narrative to the very contemporary setting of the Rio de Janeiro carnival, a 'movement of proximation' in Gérard Genette's terms (1997: 304). The Orpheus of this film is a musician of considerable skill, as well as being a ticket conductor on the Rio tram network. Early on we see him repurchasing his guitar from the pawnshop, one of the film's numerous allusions to the poverty in which this modern mythical hero resides: he lives in a shanty town or *favela* on the hillside overlooking the Brazilian capital. At one point, he persuades two young boys, whose gaze in some sense provides the audience's point of view in this film, that his guitar, which is the equivalent to Orpheus's lyre, has the power to make the sun rise and set. The sartorial association of Orpheus with the sun in this film draws on the suggestion in many versions of the myth that Orpheus was the son of Apollo. At the end, when Orpheus has been murdered by a jealous horde of women as myth dictates, the sun becomes a symbol of regeneration. One of the boys picks up the guitar, plays the refrain associated with Orpheus, and the sun starts to rise. At this very moment, a young girl dressed in white joins him and begins to dance, instructing the young guitarist that he is now Orpheus. Eurydice was dressed in white when we first saw her, so the suggestion is that Orpheus and Eurydice live on beyond death through transmission of their love down the generations, not least via the numerous retellings of their story. There is a self-consciousness throughout *Black Orpheus* that theirs is a pre-existent narrative, an old story. A marriage registrar jokingly tells Orpheus, persuaded by his fiancée Mira to obtain a marriage licence, that his bride-to-be's name should be Eurydice, and when Orpheus first meets Eurydice at her cousin's place, he laughs, 'Wonderful, I have loved you for a thousand years ... it's a very old story'. There is a sense in which their names predestine their tragic fate. This Orpheus and Eurydice cannot escape the fate of their forebears. Their story is doomed to repeat itself.

This act of artistic repetition is, however, highly specific in cultural, temporal, and geographical terms. The *mise-en-scène* of *Black Orpheus* provides a striking version of the mythic underworld. The entire film revolves around the passion and frenzy of the Rio carnival, as did the Brazilian play by Vinicius de Moraes, *Orfeu da Conceição* (1956), which was the film's source. As well as invoking the familiar associations in the wake of the influential theories of Mikhail Bakhtin (see Bakhtin 1984 [1968]; Dentith 1995) on the temporary release of carnival from the harsh poverty-stricken realities of everyday Rio, the day's revelries provide an obvious parallel to the Bacchic intoxication of the women in the myth of Orpheus. The audience becomes as swept up in the passion and excitement of the moment as the participants, the soundscape of the film ensuring that from the opening credits the penetrating drumbeat of the carnival procession pervades ears and minds. Eurydice is pursued through the crowds and revellers of carnival by a figure in the skeletal costume of Death to the tram terminus where Orpheus usually works and where she first met him at the start of the film. Playing on the word 'terminus', part of the film's texture of verbal puns, the tram depot provides the dark space in which she meets her fate: the ominous red lighting and threatening buzzing of the electric cables adding to the sense of doom. Next we witness an ambulance speeding through the city streets with Death riding post. It enters a road tunnel, a modern evocation of Charon the ferryman taking people across the River Styx into the underworld: the point of no return as the Orpheus myth makes doubly clear.

On the hillsides and slopes, we see the sprawled-out bodies of drunken revellers, the fall-out of carnival's excess, and it is no coincidence that they resemble corpses, the lost souls of the underworld. 'Carnival is over', as one police officer informs them. *Black Orpheus* is simultaneously strikingly original and referential: this urban vision of the 'underworld' owes much, for example, to Jean Cocteau's cinematic reimagining of the Orpheus myth in post-war Paris in the renowned *Orphée* (1950).

It is the aptly named Hermes, the blind man who earlier gave Eurydice directions to the city on her arrival in Rio, who informs Orpheus of his new love's demise. Hermes is, in mythological terms, a messenger, but also the god of transport, hence his association with the space of the tram depot. He is by tradition the spiritual guide to the underworld and it is he who takes Orpheus to find Eurydice at the local mortuary. Section 12 of the mortuary proves, quite literally, the site of 'lost souls'. There are no bodies to be found, only a janitor drowning in stacks of paperwork. In this way, there is a quiet but disturbing analogy with the anonymous world of modern bureaucracy and the sad fate of missing persons in South America throughout much of the twentieth century. Travelling down stairwells lit by a reddish hue, Orpheus passes a barking guard dog: this is Cerberus, the many-headed canine who guards the gates of the underworld. Eventually, Orpheus finds himself in a room of white-robed singers and dancers in a state of trance or intoxication, a version of a *voodoo* ritual, an underworld of drug-induced states. Orpheus's song is invited to conjure Eurydice and he does hear her voice, but on the fatal turn he sees only an old woman acting as a medium for her words. Orpheus's abject sense of loss is articulated in the sociological terms alluded to elsewhere: 'I am poorer than the poorest negro' is the translation in the 1950s subtitles. Emphasizing the end of carnival, we observe Orpheus carrying Eurydice's corpse through streets being cleaned by refuse trucks, the debris of the night visible all around him.

Only music seems to provide a means of endurance at the film's close, surviving seemingly beyond the temporary timeframe of carnival, and in some ways outlasting even the fixing stone sculptures of the lovers which return in the closing credits. The story of Orpheus and Eurydice has undoubtedly continued through the ages and across cultures, perhaps endorsing earlier claims to the universality of myth. Any claim to universality, however, runs the concomitant risk of de-historicizing the particular choices of the individual work of art. The music of *Black Orpheus* is, after all, as located and specific as the Brazilian carnival that provides its central spectacle, and the roots of both these practices in the complex legacy of Portuguese colonialism deserve acknowledgement. There is certainly a case to be made, then, for the structural adaptability of certain archetypal stories – this is the essence of structuralist readings in both literature and anthropology, after all – but we must, as readers and spectators, remain alert to the specific contexts, political, cultural, and aesthetic, of each new version. *Black Orpheus* has itself been reworked in recent years by the Brazilian director Carlos Diegues as *Orfeu* (1999). In this version, the carnival and *favela* settings are retained (as is Jobim's music for the original film), but, in the crucial movement of proximity to specific contemporary concerns, Death in millennial Brazil is a local drug-dealer. The love-story of Orpheus and Eurydice is 'universal', then, and yet the threats to this particular Orpheus and Eurydice on the Rio streets are deliberately, and shockingly, (re)contextualized.

The mythic paradigm provided in *Black Orpheus* and Diegues's *Orfeu* is that in the midst of the everyday, art can, albeit temporarily, be transcendent. It is a view shared by Baz Luhrmann's 2001 film *Moulin Rouge*. In his magic realist evocation of 1890s Paris and Montmartre's infamous Moulin Rouge nightclub, Luhrmann produces a tour-de-force of filmmaking. *Moulin Rouge* is a full-blown musical which signals its origins in the great Hollywood musical films by means of visual allusions to Busby Berkeley and Fred Astaire, as well as to more avant-garde musicals such as Bob Fosse's *Cabaret*. But *Moulin Rouge* is also a postmodern reinvention of the genre. Postmodernism, as well as evincing an interest in intertextuality, has displayed a penchant for pastiche and quotation as simultaneous acts of recreation and fragmentation (Hoesterey 2001; Sim 2001). Luhrmann carefully researched his *fin-de-siècle* Parisian *mise-en-scène* and the history of the Moulin Rouge, but deliberately ruptured the historical recreation of the same by selecting a soundtrack from the 1970s–1990s. In a similarly disjunctive mode, costumes in the film are painstakingly copied from the contemporaneous paintings and sketches of La Goulue and Jane Avril by Henri de Toulouse-Lautrec made at the Moulin Rouge, and yet are worn by singers and dancers performing the works of David Bowie, T-Rex, Nirvana, Elton John, and Madonna. There is a deliberate clash of periods and contexts, drawing instructive parallels between the excesses of the late twentieth century and the previous *fin-de-siècle*.

A further diachronic parallel is implicit in Luhrmann's aesthetic: the Bohemian artistes of Montmartre are described as the 'children of the revolution'. Not only does this enable Luhrmann to play Marc Bolan's song of the same name, but it evokes the 1960s peace movement. The Indian and exotic aspects of the play-within-the film created by the English writer Christian evoke 1890s Paris and its interest in the exotic, the 1960s flirtation with eastern religion, and the 1990s explosion of Bollywood film aesthetics into the Hollywood mainstream. Bollywood, as noted earlier, is a genre partly determined by its processes of appropriation. Bollywood aesthetics are, then, ideally suited to Luhrmann's postmodern directorial style, but they carry more than purely artistic resonance in this film, reaching as they do to the film's investment at its heart in the adaptation of myth and musical for the modern era, and its specific interest in the 'timeless' and 'timely' story of Orpheus and Eurydice.

When we first enter the model-world of Paris in the film, Toulouse Lautrec is singing at the window of the fake windmill that provided the façade to the real Moulin Rouge. The camera then zooms across the cityscape to the entrance to the village of Montmartre, which is marked by a hell-mouth gateway, resonant of those used on the medieval stages and scaffolds of mystery plays, and in turn conjuring images from the paintings of Hieronymous Bosch. Luhrmann's reference is again a literal one: the hell-mouth entrance to the *Cabaret d'enfer* (Cabaret of Hell) that stood opposite the Moulin Rouge on the Place Blanche, with its infamous façade of falling figures of damned souls (Milner 1988: 140). The hellish associations of the night-club are implied by this image, a reading further strengthened by the words of Christian's father who warns him against entering this dangerous world: 'Turn away from this village of sin, this Sodom and Gomorrah.' Christian's overlaid first person narrative confirms the connection: 'Moulin Rouge. A nightclub, a dancehall, and a bordello, ruled over by Harold Zidler, the kingdom of night-time pleasure where the rich and powerful come to play with the young and beautiful creatures of the underworld.' If Christian is our Orpheus, descending into the seductive underworld of Zidler's club –

the real owner of the Moulin Rouge was Charles Zidler (Hanson and Hanson 1956: 128) – where the dominant colour palette is fiery oranges and reds, and where momentarily the lit oars of the windmill resemble red pitchforks in the sky, then his Eurydice is the courtesan and performer Satine. Christian and Satine's great passion is expressed musically throughout the film and is encapsulated in their duet 'Come what may', with its central lyric 'I will love you till my dying day'. Their love is, however, doomed, as fated and temporary in the material world of the nightclub as that of their mythic forebears: Satine, unbeknownst either to Christian or herself, is dying.

The myth of Orpheus and Eurydice is only one of several informing subtexts for *Moulin Rouge*: Giacomo Puccini's opera *La Bohème*, set in the Paris wintertime of the 1830s, is another crucial focus of allusion. In that opera, which Luhrmann went on to direct in New York following the filming of *Moulin Rouge*, a group of students, artists, musicians, singers, and writers, struggle to survive in a Paris garret. Rodolfo, an author, falls in love with Mimi. This couple forms the focus of several duets in the opera in a manner akin to the Christian-Satine union in *Moulin Rouge*. Mimi is suffering from tuberculosis and her death provides the opera's poignant finale. The parallels with *Moulin Rouge*, which signals its indebtedness to opera as well as musical in the structures and references of its soundtrack, are self-evident. *La Bohème* shares the nineteenth-century Parisian locale of Luhrmann's film in a way that Orpheus's mythic landscape never can. But it is in the culminating performance of Christian's play-within-a-film about the penniless sitar-player that the Orpheus and Eurydice narrative resurfaces with full force.

Informed by Zidler that she is dying of consumption and that her suitor, the duke, intends to kill Christian, Satine casts her lover off in a self-sacrificing effort to save his life. Subsequently we witness his painful efforts to gain re-entry to the underworld of the nightclub, only to be cast in the gutter by the duke's henchmen. Finally he obtains access and, breaking the frame of the performance, walks onstage to reject Satine, who he believes has betrayed him for financial gain. As he walks away down the theatre's central aisle, Satine begins to sing their song. In a vital twist on Orpheus's persuasion of the underworld through the power of his song, Christian is brought back to Satine by the power of emotion implicit in her voice.

Black Orpheus and *Moulin Rouge* appear to embody the truth of Rilke's claim in the epigraph to this section that 'it's Orpheus, whenever there is song'. What then is a reader to make of a novel that features neither music nor song, nor signals its Orphic connections in the ways that Camus and Luhrmann do? Graham Swift's *The Light of Day* is, I suggest, an Orpheus appropriation by way of 'critical proxy' as Chantal Zabus terms it (2002: 121). It is not something the creator has signalled to us in any explicit fashion. As earlier discussions of Swift's intertextual style have indicated, his refusal to cite sources explicitly has troubled critics (see Chapter 2). Swift's work is not dependent on his sources to the extent that it fails to make sense without knowledge of the appropriation in operation. Lack of foreknowledge of the resonance of the Orpheus story will not collapse any reading of *The Light of Day*, or its intricately related themes of exile, detection, and love. Nevertheless, the reader who approaches the novel with a sense of the subtextual undertow provided by the Orpheus myth releases the opportunity for additional interpretations which can only enrich understanding of the novel. Swift's decision, for example, to mention, a few chapters from the close, the cave network that exists under Chislehurst is reasonable enough in its own right. But if the reader is aware that in both Virgil's and Ovid's versions of the myth, Orpheus descends to the underworld by means of a cave, then this simple connection of caves with underworlds, and by extension with the Orpheus and Eurydice story, brings myth into the everyday world of this novel in exciting ways. What we are doing by recognizing the mythic undertow to Swift's novel is expanding the potential network of meanings available to the active and interactive reader. It is a classic example of the way in which this form of embedded intertextuality, one that does not signal or demand an intertextual interpretative framework for any reading as certain explicit adaptations necessarily do, depends crucially upon the reader's recognition of the subtexts and intertexts involved. It is a working example of Wolfgang Iser's theory of reader-reception: manipulation and control is certainly exerted by the text upon the reader, but the reading process remains reliant upon different and differing modes of collaboration between reader and narrative in the production of meanings (Iser 2001: 179–84).

What Swift's novel ultimately proves is that it is often in the mundane, quotidian world of supermarkets, crematoria, and suburban kitchens that the deepest, darkest emotions are at work. Swift's title, *The Light of Day*, a phrase that contributes the closing words of the novel, has multiple connotations. The first person narrator is George Webb, a failed policeman turned private detective, regularly charged by suspicious wives with the task of proving their husbands' adultery by bringing to 'the light of day' firm evidence, frequently in the form of photographs. Photography is a medium whose ability both to see clearly and to occlude has troubled Swift in a previous novel, *Out of this World*, about a photo war-journalist. Here the photographic images bring the fact of adultery to the light of day while being unable to tell the full story of relationships. This in turn becomes a metaphor for George's narrative, which is fragmentary and incomplete in many respects. He acknowledges that there are some things that simply cannot be said or revealed.

If George puns openly on his forename, stressing that his sordid profession means he is no 'saint George', it is his surname that carries the active intertextual and collaborational reader into the mythic realms I am proposing. Web(b)s and weaving carry potent meaning in classical texts from Homer's *Odyssey*, with Penelope weaving and unweaving her father-in-law's shroud in an effort to fend off suitors during her husband's nineteen-years' absence, to Ovid's *Metamorphoses*, where Arachne's tapestry provides the space of several inset stories in a manner akin to Orpheus's song.

Henry James's *Washington Square* offers a striking, and disturbing, version of this in the nineteenth century when at the end of the novel Catherine takes up 'her morsel of fancy-work ... for life, as it were' (James 1984 [1880]: 220). The webs of connection that Swift's novel encourages carry us as readers across a line from the everyday into the underworlds and recesses of myth. In the same way that the novel imbues clichés and commonplace phrases, such as 'crossing a line', 'missing persons', 'safe-as-houses', and 'time to kill', with new relevance, so the mythic subtexts to the narrative encourage us to reassess the surfaces of what we are reading.

For George, the underworld in which his Eurydice is trapped is the British prison system. The focus of his loyal, even obsessive, affection is Sarah, a former client. She, as we learn only gradually from George's digressive narrative, employed the private detective to ensure that her husband really was finishing a relationship with their Croatian *au pair*.

But Sarah murdered her husband at the very moment when he seemed to have returned to the folds of their married life. This is an act for which a full explanation is never provided and yet about which there is endless speculation within the pages of the text. The narrative is retrospective; looking back over a period of two years, George's troubled recollections and half-recollections are just one example of many gestures of looking back in this novel. As it was for Orpheus, this is an action fraught with danger and loss, revealing painful truths, as well as suppressions of the truth. This is a text in which everything is not brought into the clear light of day; motives and actions remain shrouded in darkness, emotions unspoken, issues unresolved. Bob, Sarah's husband, enacts several poignant gestures, real and imagined, of looking back in the course of the narrative. Leaving the flat in which he had installed his mistress, he looks back, as if remembering the previous passionate encounters the space had contained: 'He walked round to his driver's door and before getting in, and with an odd quick wrench of the head, looked up, looked round, looked back' (Swift 2003: 126). Later, driving behind the car in which Bob is transporting his mistress to the airport, George wonders if Bob looks back at his hospital workplace (141). Following the airport lounge separation, Bob returns to the flat one last time. As with Orpheus, this could be interpreted as his fatal mistake. The gesture of looking back makes him late returning to the house he shares with Sarah. This in turn seems to plant in her mind a sense of doubt as to how the future will be between them, possibly provoking the fatal stabbing, though the narrative never clarifies any of these points.

What is clear from this reading is that the appropriation of Orpheus's story is mediated through at least two characters. Both Bob and George function as Orpheus; both descend into underworlds; both are engaged in the perilous action of looking back. In a similar vein, Swift's recreation of the 'underworld' is present in several of the carefully mapped spaces of this novel. If the topography of London is all too tangible in Swift's deliberately prosaic narrative, the shadow-world of myth provides an alternative psychic map. It is as if Swift's narrator resides in the same limbo as Bendrix the first person narrator of Graham Greene's *The End of the Affair* (1951), and another retrospective narrator suffering from an obsessive, lost, love: 'If this book of mine fails to take a straight course, it is because I am lost in a strange region: I have no map' (Greene 2001: 50). Swift's sparing dialogue has often been compared to Greene's. Intriguingly, Hermione Lee has suggested Greene's novel as another possible intertext for *The Light of Day*. In both texts the female protagonist, obsessed over by the first person narrator, is called Sarah; both are retrospective narratives of love and loss; and yet it is as if, states Lee, Greene's comic marginal character of Parkis the detective has, in Swift's novel, been given centre stage (2003: 9). It might be added that in Greene's and Swift's novels the figure of Sarah remains distanced from both reader and narrator, an enigma at the heart of the text. The same can be said of Eurydice's participation in versions of her myth: often silenced completely in the underworld sequences, she has been sidelined in many subsequent reworkings of the story, placed back in the shadows by artistic self-interest in the figure of Orpheus. Revisiting the Orpheus myth, however, several feminist writers and critics have striven to give Eurydice a voice, including H.D. in her eponymous poem of 1917 where her heroine castigates Orpheus's 'arrogance' ('Eurydice', l. 6. Cited in Miles 1999: 159–62) in looking back and thus assigning her to the darkness of Hades a second time, when as Virgil so poignantly points out she was 'on the lip of / Daylight' (Virgil 1983: 125). This is an example of what Rachel Blau DuPlessis describes as the 'poetics of rupture and critique' that myth is constantly subjected to by women writers (1985: 32).

There are recurring images of darkness in *The Light of Day*: George is constantly positioned in the shadows or in spaces only partly penetrated by light, from his office to his car, to various police interview rooms, to the prison waiting room where he visits his Eurydice, these latter encounters providing the rhythm and ritual of his otherwise oddly empty existence. Leaving the crematorium, where he has taken flowers to mark the anniversary of Bob's death, he describes re-entering the road system as launching himself 'back into the world'; later, the queue of prison visitors are to all intents and purposes souls in limbo. The underworld is everywhere and everyday in this novel. What the mention of the caves beneath Chislehurst brings to bear in the closing chapters is a mythic world of intense emotion and irreversible actions: 'The echoes, the maze of tunnels, the stories of ghosts. The feeling that you might never get back into the light' (Swift, 2003: 237). The narrative ends with George hoping for the day when Sarah will be released into his arms, into 'the clear light of day'. This can be read optimistically, but any reader aware of the Orpheus and Eurydice myth cannot help but be afraid for the way this story might unfold. The familiar paradigms of myth allow Swift to leave much unsaid.

Ovidian metamorphoses and Orphic narratives have serviced a very diverse range of cultural appropriations. In some, though not all, of these reworkings that interrelationship is explicit; in others the intertextuality operates in a subterranean mode, occurring beneath the surface narrative. In all instances an awareness of the informing myths alters our responses as readers to the adaptive and appropriative texts. Mythic paradigms provide the reader or spectator with a series of familiar reference points and a set of expectations which the novelist, artist, director, playwright, composer, or poet can rely upon as an instructive shorthand, while simultaneously exploiting, twisting, and relocating them in newly creative ways, and in newly resonant contexts. Frequently, political commitment informs and influences these acts of re-creation, for, as DuPlessis notes, 'To change a story signals a dissent from social norms as well as narrative forms' (1985: 20). We are entering, therefore, the tricky domain of authorial 'intention', a world which in some respects Barthes's notion of the reader as an active creator of meanings sought to eschew, and yet it seems inescapable in any genuine study of the motives involved in adaptational art (Patterson 1987: 135–46). In such works of adaptation or appropriation, political awareness, and even complicity, is frequently required on the part of the reader or spectator receiving the recreated text or performance, although there are also important distinctions between responses to adaptations in different generic modes, to film, song, or literature, for example. There are, then, crucial issues raised by all of this to do with the relationship and interaction between writer, reader or spectator, and genre that the multiple reoccurrences of myth throw into relief. Each moment of reception is individual and distinct, albeit governed by manifold conventions and traditions, by prior knowledges and previous texts: the old story becomes in this respect a very new one, told – and read – for the first time.

5

'OTHER VERSIONS' OF FAIRY TALE AND FOLKLORE

The overlap between the genres of myth, legend, folklore, and fairy tales has exercised many scholars (Sale 1978: 23). The well-known story of Robin Hood, for example, moves at various times from exhibiting the conventions of legend to serving as local folklore, while also invoking the witches and fairies from fairy tale (Knight 2003). Fairy tales, with their interest in dysfunctional family structures and personal and civic rites of passage, have much in common with their mythological counterparts. All these forms have also been interpreted from the varying standpoints of anthropology, social history, cultural studies, structuralism, feminism, psychoanalysis, and psychology. What they offer are archetypal stories available for re-use and recycling by different ages and cultures. Fairy tale and folklore do, however, possess a very specific set of signifiers and symbolic systems that are worth examining in their own right. Shakespeare, a prime example, as we have already seen, of a cultural repository of archetypal characters and plotlines, dipped into the folk genre of fairy tale as a stimulus for his drama: *King Lear* and *Cymbeline*, for example, both have roots in this form. *Cymbeline* reconstitutes the figure of the wicked stepmother, while *Lear* reworks a folklore storyline of a father and his three daughters, two malign or 'ugly' sisters, and one good and virtuous child.

One of the reasons fairy tale and folklore serve as cultural treasuries to which we endlessly return is that their stories and characters seem to transgress established social, cultural, geographical, and temporal boundaries. They are eminently adaptable into new circumstances and contexts, making themselves available for 'other versions' (Atkinson 1997: 348). Writers, artists, and directors as diverse as Salman Rushdie, Angela Carter, Paula Rego, Kate Atkinson, Walt Disney, and Jean Cocteau have all turned to the potent form of the folk story or fairy tale as inspiration for their re-imaginings, postmodernist or otherwise. Recent comic, even parodic, versions of the fairy tale include the hugely popular animated *Shrek* films (2001; 2004) and Stephen Sondheim's 1987 musical, *Into the Woods*. Both of these are, like the dark, suggestive paintings of artist Paula Rego, an attempt to resist the so-called 'Disneyfication' of the form. Walt Disney's animated film versions of *Snow White and the Seven Dwarves, Cinderella, Sleeping Beauty*, and *Beauty and the Beast*, among others, with their explicit stress on happy endings, usually consisting for their female protagonists in marriage and the finding of their personal Prince Charming, have had a profound influence on modern understandings of the form. Nevertheless, these rich repositories of stories have also become a focus for scholarly interrogation; Marina Warner, to cite just one prominent example, is a veritable historian of the form (see, for example, Warner 1994), a fact which has influenced her fictional as well as non-fictional output.

Fairy tales are stories that are essentially variations on particular narrative types. This suggestion brings into the frame the disciplinary concerns of anthropology and the related approaches of structuralist thought and analysis. Structuralism finds much value in analysing the myths and tales of specific cultures but also in identifying the common existence of certain tales, types, and paradigmatic structures across cultures. The work of Claude Lévi-Strauss and Tzvetan Todorov, among others, has had considerable influence on those critics who study the presence of mythical and folkloric types in literature ranging from the plays of Shakespeare to magic realism (see Lévi-Strauss 2001 [1978]; Todorov 1990 [1978]). In terms of the ongoing adaptation of fairy tales, the recurrence of particular narrative types and structures in new, culturally embedded contexts raises the same dichotomy between universality and a politicized subject position that Roland Barthes's *Mythologies* was seen to grapple with in the previous chapter's examinations of myth (1993 [1972]). In turn, as we shall see in this chapter, structuralism has been inflected by the findings of psychoanalysis. In Sigmund Freud's theory of *unheimlich*, or the 'uncanny', for example, it is possible to identify a version of the compulsion to repetition, the desire to return to or recreate a text, story or paradigm, as both a refusal and rehearsal of loss and as an effort to contain anxiety (Freud 1963 [1919]; Garber 1987). The darker subtexts of many fairy stories, as with myths, raise spectres of incest, familial violence, and monstrousness that might elsewhere be seen as the stuff of dreams and nightmares.

If fairy tale and folklore make themselves particularly available for continuous re-creation and rewriting it is partly because of their essential abstraction from a specific context: 'Although the content of the fairy tale may record the real lives of the anonymous poor with sometimes uncomfortable fidelity ... the form of the fairy tale is not usually constructed so as to invite the audience to share a sense of lived experience' (Carter 1990: xi). The castles, towers, villages, forests, monsters, beasts, ogres, and princesses of fairy tale exist seemingly nowhere and yet everywhere in terms of applicability and relevance. But a detectable counter-movement in twentieth-century reworkings of the form can be located in the desire to tie the stories back into a social, even socio-historical, context, constituting in some respects an attempt to rationalize their magic. Christopher Wallace's novel *The Pied Piper's Poison* (1998) reconsiders the familiar children's tale of the Pied Piper of Hamelin who helps to rid a Northern European village of an infestation of rats, harbingers of life-threatening plague, by means of his seductive music, but who, when his payment is revoked by the town, returns to entice away the children, and therefore the symbolic economic future of the community. Deploying the narrative structure of an academic research paper cited within a retirement speech by a doctor, Wallace's novel self-consciously asserts and queries the value and reliability of expert testimony. The academic article is a reconsideration of the Hamelin story. Rejecting the fantasy element of the folk tale as handed down through the generations, its author finds a disturbingly material explanation for the events suggested in the story of the Pied Piper. Retrieving the socio-historical context of the Thirty Years War in Europe in the 1630s and 1640s, the essay suggests that Hamelin was not besieged by rats, although in a grain-growing community they were an omnipresent feature. Instead it speculates, and the speculative nature, the unreliability, of the historical archive is stressed at various points, that the town was under siege from a band of Spanish soldiers. It is these 'rats' that the Pied Piper offers to rid Hamelin of. The description of the Piper himself extends the mode of social realism that Wallace applies to the tale, as he considers the possible reasons behind the name:

> 'Pied' could conceivably be a corruption of the French '*à pied*', meaning 'on foot', indicating that this man was by nature a traveller. It could also imply the style of clothing he wore, 'pied' meaning mottled or spotted, with the kind of bright and bold colour associated with a jester or clown. Finally, the word could be a corruption of his real name, particularly if this was Arabic in origin and therefore difficult for an uneducated German speaker to pronounce.
>
> (Wallace 1998: 160)

The narrative here emulates the discursive style of the rational, scientific age, offering definitions and explanations. The latter explanation also gestures towards a cultural awareness of the social and class structures that provide the shaping forces to the supposedly abstract forms of fairy tale, folk tale, and the related genre of nursery rhyme. The Pied Piper is, in Wallace's analysis, or at least the analysis of the academic in his fiction, an outsider, possibly an Eastern migrant worker in seventeenth-century Europe. This gesture is towards the fact that many fairy tales exhibit a deep rooted anxiety about the figure of the incomer, the outsider, the person or creature from elsewhere. Marxist interpretations of tales such as *Rumplestiltskin*, for example, suggest that it tries to work through a threat to the common means of production through spinning in many Northern European villages in the Middle Ages.

It does not take much of a leap of the imagination to see how this tale could be redeployed in an analysis of the twenty-first century European paranoia surrounding migrant workers and asylum seekers. Jack Zipes has talked of the 'universal community' implied by fairy tale (1994: 5), but his Marxist analyses of the tales also stress their specific historical and social contexts. For Zipes, *Rumplestiltskin* is 'about the merchant capitalist intensification of linen manufacture and the appropriation of the means of production through which [the heroine] would normally establish her quality and win her man' (1994: 68).

Similarly, Wallace's cultural materialist analysis of the Pied Piper's mythology serves to shed light on the second focus time period in his novel, the Second World War, when other forms of social hardship and threat were being faced by European communities akin to those of Hamelin. As well as paralleling the two conflicts via his double time-scheme, Wallace, again via his subject academic Arthur Lee, finds a troubling parallel to the folk tale in the twentieth-century wartime practice of torture. In this version of the Pied Piper legend, the children are not seduced by the melodies played by a travelling minstrel to leave the village; they are eaten by hallucinating townsfolk in an extreme state of famine, people reduced quite literally to the condition of rats by their situation. Any metamorphosis in this tale proves chillingly explicable in terms of hunger and insanity. In turn, the cruelties inflicted upon neighbouring communities during the Second World War are brought into disturbing focus. In the end our need to weave stories around terrible events is seen to be a remarkably stable need in human society; we displace reality in order to survive, and to evade the awful truth that the capacity for cruelty is within us all. Except in our imaginations, there is no Pied Piper to scapegoat.

The language of scapegoating reintroduces the anthropological roots and concerns of structuralist theory. In a manner akin to Shakespeare and myth, then, the impulse towards re-visioning fairy tales can be linked to specific theoretical movements, but, as well as charting the rise of anthropology as a discipline in the twentieth century, the fairy tale carries the weight of significance ascribed to it by the emergent modes of psychology and psychoanalysis. A seminal work in this respect is Bruno Bettelheim's *The Uses of Enchantment: The Meaning and Importance of Fairy Tales*, first published in 1975. Influenced by the work of Sigmund Freud and Carl Jung, Bettelheim explored the 'psychological significance of the folk fairy tale' (1975: 5). In a manner that shares much of its method with Wallace's rationalization of the Pied Piper story, Bettelheim suggested that many such tales were a means of working through traumatic experiences caused by the social visitations of plague, famine, and warfare, or by the sexual and social pressures created by puberty and adolescence. It is notable how many of the protagonists of fairy tales find themselves on a threshold between childhood and adulthood, between innocence and experience in sexual terms: *Snow*

White, Little Red Riding Hood, and *Sleeping Beauty* all conform to this archetype. As Bettelheim observes: 'fairy tales depict in imaginary and symbolic form the essential steps in growing up and achieving an independent existence' (1975: 73). Feminist writers have found a particularly rich source of material in fairy tale for this reason. Kate Atkinson's self-aware narrator in *Human Croquet* instructs her readers early on that it is her birthday, and a significant one at that: 'It's the first day of April and it's my birthday, my sixteenth – the mythic one, the legendary one, the traditional age for spindles to start pricking and suitors to come calling and a host of other symbolic sexual imagery to suddenly manifest itself …' (Atkinson 1997: 23). The date of April Fools' Day must give readers pause in that Isobel, with her postmodern awareness of the available readings of fairy tale, is also likely to be an unreliable narrator. Nevertheless, this statement alerts readers to the manifold ways in which Atkinson's text, as already indicated in the previous chapter, will engage in a rich intertextual relationship with Shakespeare, Ovidian mythology, and fairy tales ranging from *Sleeping Beauty* through *Cinderella* to *Little Red Riding Hood* and *Hansel and Gretel*.

Atkinson is especially interested in the fairy tale's invocation of the family both as an ideal and as an entity capable of horrific dysfunctionality. She also finds Shakespearean plays a rich source in this respect. The interplay of sibling rivalry and dependency that features in tales such as *Cinderella* and *Hansel and Gretel* figures in Isobel and Charles's relationship in the face of the loss of their mother and the temporary absence of their father. This is also a common motif in fairy tale, one that allows the 'orphan' a free space for experience. *Human Croquet* is a narrative awash with stepmothers, not all of them archetypally wicked, parental failures and absences, dysfunctional familial relationships, and sexual threat. Although in the early stages of the novel Isobel and Charles appear to nurse the hope that their mother Eliza might still be alive, partly signified by the Cinderella-esque shoe which they hope will one day be filled by the foot of their returned mother, we later realize that they have repressed the fact of finding their mother's bloody corpse in a woodland during an ill-fated family picnic. Eliza was, in fact, murdered with the missing shoe from the pair.

The deployment of the fairy tale (and quasi-Shakespearean) setting of the forest is another important thread in Atkinson's complex narrative. Isobel and Charles become in this moment the 'babes in the wood' of

Hansel and Gretel: 'She was so hungry that she would have eaten a gingerbread tile or a piece of striped candy window-frame, even though she knew the consequences' (1997: 130–1). The telling point in this quotation is that Isobel 'knew the consequences'; it is this knowing attitude adopted by the narrative towards its intertextual source that causes us persistently to question any possibility of the traditional fairy tale happy ending for these characters. Isobel recognizes as much in her analysis of the masculine presences in her adolescent life: 'It seems men fall into one of several categories – there are the weak fathers, the ugly brothers, the evil villains, the heroic woodcutters and, of course, the handsome princes – none of which seems entirely satisfactory somehow' (1997: 75). The sexual subtext of many fairy tales, indicated by Bettelheim's contextualization in terms of pubescence and sexual awakening, recurs in *Human Croquet*, finding its most troubling manifestation in the Baxter family. On the surface this is a textbook 'happy family' with a mother constantly baking cakes and attending to her husband's needs, but a postmodern, postfeminist reader will never be satisfied with this version of events. In fact at the heart of the Baxter family is domestic violence and incest, making all too real the novel's favourite cliché, 'Appearances can be deceptive'. Atkinson has pursued these interests in another novel, *Case Histories* (2004), which combines the generic and topographic conventions of contemporary detective fiction with fairy tale tropes and motifs.

Atkinson's *Human Croquet* with its parallel worlds and time-travelling motifs owes much to the genres of fantasy and science fiction as well as Shakespeare, Ovid, and fairy tale. Her narrative technique has, therefore, much in common with the mode of 'magic realism' which rose to prominence in the latter decades of the twentieth century, enjoying plural manifestations in the writings of South and Central American authors, in Eastern European art, and in feminist and postcolonial texts. The preceding chapter discussed the treatment of myth in Salman Rushdie's novels in this context and a prime influence on Rushdie and on Atkinson's version of magic realism is Angela Carter. It is undoubtedly to the genre of the fairy tale that Carter looked for her source material for the magic realist impulse in her writing:

> It is through her use of fairy-tale components that Carter disrupts the realism that [her writing] otherwise cultivates. Carter recognizes the

misogyny of the conventional fairy-tale, as well as the amenability of fairy-tales to being rewritten and disseminated in ways which enshrine particular (especially patriarchal) social codes; but it is through this realization that Carter reclaims the fairy-tale as a medium for the feminist writer.

(Head 2002: 92)

Sarah Gamble suggests that for Carter 'appropriation and adaptation is really what the fairy tale is all about' (1997: 67), citing Carter's personal definition of the form:

The chances are, the story was put together in the form we have it, more or less out of all sorts of bits of other stories long ago and far away, and has been tinkered with, had bits added to it, lost other bits, got mixed up with other stories, until our informant herself has tailored the story personally to suit an audience ... or, simply, to suit herself.

(Carter 1990: x)

This is a brilliant summary of the operations of *bricolage*.

Suiting herself and her audience, Carter's re-visionary fairy tales exhibit a deep-seated interest in the sexual subtexts identified by Bettelheim. The collection of short stories that make up her 1979 collection *The Bloody Chamber*, and which rewrite *Beauty and the Beast*, *Puss in Boots*, *Little Red Riding Hood*, and the story of Bluebeard's castle (in the title story), are awash with descriptions of the human body and the sexual act, as well as female menstruation, which for Carter is the epitome of the sexual threshold on which the female protagonists of fairy tale stand. In 'The Company of Wolves', for example, the unnamed Red Riding Hood's metonymic 'scarlet shawl' signifies not only her traditional literary identity to the reader but becomes further emblematic of the sexual limen on which she is poised; it is 'the colour of poppies, the colour of sacrifices, the colour of her menses ...' (1995 [1979]: 117). 'The Company of Wolves' takes place on the calendrical limen or threshold of the winter solstice; Carter loved to use these 'hinge' moments of the year as the space for possibility in her revisionary writings.

This particular version of 'Little Red Riding Hood' revels in the heroine's wilful sexual coupling with the wolf rather than the violent devouring that her grandmother is subjected to. Carter finds in the fairy tale wide potential for realizing the liberation as well as constraint of women, freeing several of her heroines from the restrictive trajectory of marriage in the process. As Lorna Sage eloquently described it, in Carter's hands 'The monsters and the princesses lose their places in the old script ...' (1994: 39). But Carter's feminocentric tales do not substitute some naïve version of the female hero for the contained heroines of her sources. In many of the tales the female protagonists prove complicit in their entrapment, travelling, seemingly without question, into 'the unguessable country of marriage' (7). In 'The Bloody Chamber', for example, part of the heroine-narrator's steep learning curve is a recognition that she was seduced by the wealth of her mysterious husband, who the reader soon comes to recognize as the murderous Bluebeard from the clues provided by the pornographic literature in his personal library and those all-too-significant keys. This story of suppressed violence against women has, of course, haunted much feminist fiction: in the twentieth century, inspiring, for example, Margaret Atwood's *Bluebeard's Egg and other short stories* and Alice Hoffman's *Blue Diary* and in the nineteenth century hovering just beneath the surface of Charlotte Brontë's *Jane Eyre*. In Carter's vivid reimagining, the marquis's gold bathroom taps and the fine fabrics he fills his bride's wardrobe with seem to muffle her ability to question his poor track record in previous marriages. It is in the figure of the indomitable mother who rescues her daughter at the close that Carter allows herself a dramatic feminist interpolation into the heart of the Bluebeard myth, actively regendering Charles Perrault's saviour brothers from the seventeenth-century French version of the tale.

During her career, Carter edited two collections of fairy tales for the Virago publishing house (1990 and 1992). In 1977 she also translated Perrault's influential collection *Histoires ou contes du temps passé* (1697). She was a scholar as well as an adaptor of the form; fairy tale was clearly a paradigmatic genre throughout her *oeuvre*, appearing in various shapes and forms in novels including *The Magic Toyshop* (1967), in which according to Dominic Head: 'the challenge to the fairy-tale is conducted in an ambivalent spirit. Where the fairy-tales of the brothers Grimm or Perrault suppress their subtext of sexuality, Carter makes the emerging sexuality of her fifteen-year-old protagonist Melanie the narrative's driving force' (2002: 92–3). Postfeminist versions of fairy tales also figure in her short story collections, including *Fireworks* (1988) and the posthumously published *American Ghosts and Old World Wonders* (1994). The latter includes not one but three alternative versions of the Cinderella myth, as if to emphasize Carter's awareness of the revisionary potential of these texts.

The engaged and intrusive narrator of 'Ashputtle or The Mother's Ghost, Three Versions of One Story' discusses the possibility of adopting a new perspective on the Cinderella myth: 'you could easily take the story away from Ashputtle and centre it on the mutilated sisters ...' (1994: 110). Carter is deliberately restoring the violence of earlier versions of the story, scenes in which the stepmother of this tale mutilates her own daughters' feet in an effort to force them to fit the prince's shoe. In context the image is a disturbing one, suggesting the desperation surrounding the marriage potential of daughters in earlier societies, but Carter suggests an equally troubling modern parallel in rituals of footbinding and female circumcision (1994: 110). The narrator also ponders the father's failure to act in the face of the violence performed by his second wife on his daughter in the family home, speculating that if you made all three daughters in the story his biological daughters that would alter things: 'But it would also transform the story into something else, because it would provide motivation, and so on; it would mean I'd have to provide a past for all these people, that I would have to equip them with three dimensions ...' (110). Carter is being deliberately playful here since it is this provision of pre-history and motivation, the restoration of three dimensions, that we have seen as central to the reworkings of Shakespeare, myth, and fairy tale studied in this section and which is undoubtedly central to her own revisionary impulse.

Fairy tale and folklore have a complicated relationship to print history. While the names of Perrault, the Brothers Grimm, and Hans Christian Andersen have become virtually synonymous with fairy tales, these authors were issuing in print personalized versions of stories that had long circulated in an oral, popular cultural context. As Marina Warner has shown oral culture was also a far more feminocentric community, although both Warner and Carter are equally aware of a female precedent in print for their modern fairy tales. Mme d'Aulnoy's *Les Contes des Fées* (1697–8) disseminated in printed form a number of the stories that had been shared and circulated within French salon culture, a largely female enterprise (Zipes 1994: 20). Her tales of animal bride-grooms in particular paved the way for the story of *La belle et la bête*, which has proved a recurrent interest to Carter. In *The Bloody Chamber* as well as wolf-bridegrooms, there are two specific variations on the Beauty and the Beast tale: 'The Courtship of Mr Lyon' which has a self-consciously trite resolution in the marriage of its protagonists, and the far darker and more sexualized 'The Tiger's Bride', where, in a typical act of inversion through appropriation, Carter's Beauty does not trans-form the beast into the normative vision of a prince but rather, once the tiger-bridegroom licks off her layers of skin, becomes furred herself. In keeping with the cinematic intertextuality of so much of her prose, Carter's Gothic re-visions of this story are also indebted to Jean Cocteau's memorable film version (1945).

It is striking to note that several of the authors invoked in this analy-sis of the appropriation of fairy tale plotlines and paradigms also engage at length with Shakespeare in their writing: Atkinson with the Shakespearean comedies in *Human Croquet*, Carter with the entire Shakespearean canon in her *tour-de-force* novel *Wise Children*. Marina Warner's novel *Indigo*, already mentioned in Chapter 3 in relation to its improvisational approach to *The Tempest*, is also a text steeped in Ovidian mythology, and fairy tale. The novel is framed by the storytelling of its quasi-magical character Serafine Killabree, who is linked at various points in the narrative to the sub-Shakespearean witch Sycorax. The first story she tells, of a king, his beautiful daughter, golden-haired as in all the best fairy tales, and a fat suitor who eats oysters, both invokes the Ovidian metamorphic myth of Midas who turned objects to gold, and offers a template for understanding the relationship in the novel between the characters of Sir Anthony Everard and his spoiled daughter Xanthe and her future husband, Sy Nebris, who founds an oyster farm on the family's Caribbean landholdings. Xanthe's name means 'gilded one' in Latin, and she is also nicknamed 'Goldie' in the novel, evoking several fairy tale paradigms including the selfish and greedy Goldilocks and endless tales of sibling rivalry between sisters marked alternately 'good' and 'bad', often through the troubling epithets of light and dark hair. Xanthe's mixed-race half-sister Miranda is clearly troubled by the narra-tive implications of such literary traditions. Through her intertextual weaving of the mermaids and sea-changes of Shakespeare's *The Tempest* with those of fairy tales, Warner constructs a distinctly feminocentric narrative. It seems fitting that the novel closes with Serafine still telling and retelling stories in the style of Mother Goose and the ancient spinners of the verbal cloths of fairy tale. Mirroring the postcolonial and feminist concerns of Warner's novel, the myths and tales told by Serafine contain stories of devouring, of death, and consumption, sexual or otherwise, but they are being constantly revised, rewritten, and retold in new contexts: 'But this savage story isn't seemly for the little English girls, so Serafine has adapted it, as storytellers do' (1992: 224). This is the self-conscious appropriative art of Warner, Carter, Atkinson, and many others. They are deliberately breaking down and deconstructing the conventions of fairy tale, viewing things from a new angle. As Jack Zipes reminds us, they do this: 'in order to alter our readings of the privileged narratives that have formed a type of canon in Western culture' (1994: 157). But, as Zipes also notes, their 'postmodern revisions ... do not reassemble the fairytales that they break down into fragments into a new whole. Instead, they expose the artifice of the fairytale and make us aware that there are different ways to shape and view the stories' (1994: 157).

In the end it is the happy ending of fairy tale that is most vociferously denied, or at least self-consciously framed, by these revisionary versions. Proving once again that stasis is an unreliable model for the operations of canonical texts across cultures and time, these 'other versions' open up rather than close down possibility, offering 'not recuperation but differentiation, not the establishment of a new norm but the questioning of all norms' (Zipes 1994: 157–8; see also Zipes 1979: 177).

PART 3

ALTERNATIVE
PERSPECTIVES

6

CONSTRUCTING ALTERNATIVE
POINTS OF VIEW

It has become abundantly clear in the discussion of adaptation and appropriation in this volume that these processes are frequently, if not inevitably, political acts. While the action of reinterpretation in a new context was viewed by T. S. Eliot in 'Tradition and the Individual Talent' as a necessary, indeed highly valuable, aspect of literary creation, he was ostensibly discussing a form of relationship between intertexts that mirrored his own cultural *bricolage* of quotation and allusion in poems such as 'The Waste Land'. That 1922 poem refers, among copious other texts and influences, to John Webster's *The White Devil*, William Shakespeare's *Antony and Cleopatra*, Ovid's *Metamorphoses*, Henry James, and the poetry of Charles Baudelaire.

The relationship between intertexts and the referential process alters in significance when the appropriation extends beyond fragmentary allusion to a more sustained reworking and revision. If readers are to be alert to the comparative and contrastive relationships that Eliot regarded as crucial to the aesthetic process, it goes almost without saying that the texts cited or reworked need to be well known. They need to serve as part of a shared community of knowledge, both for the interrelationships and interplay to be identifiable and for these in turn to have the required impact on their readership. This is why, as we discussed in the introduction, adaptation and appropriation tend on the whole to operate within the parameters of an established canon, serving indeed at times to reinforce that canon by ensuring a continued interest in the original or source text, albeit in revised circumstances of understanding. To repeat Derek Attridge's formulation which was cited in the introductory discussion: 'The perpetuation of any canon is dependent in part on the references made to its earlier members by its later members ...' (1996: 169). These necessary operations within the parameters of the canon, however, need not mean that appropriations merely accept or cite their precursor text without question or critique. Indeed the study of appropriations in an academic context has in part been spurred on by the recognized ability of adaptation to respond or write back to an informing original from a new or revised political and cultural position, and by the capacity of appropriations to highlight troubling gaps, absences, and silences within the canonical texts to which they refer. Many appropriations have a joint political and literary investment in giving voice to those characters or subject-positions they perceive to have been oppressed or repressed in the original.

Attridge has usefully drawn attention to the double bind by which these subversive or counter-discursive appropriations end up by reinforcing the canonical status of the text they are taking issue with, but the important point to recall is the fact that, as readers or audience, we may never view that novel or poem or play in the same light once we have had access to the critique implicit in their appropriations. In the same way that it might be said that Charlotte Brontë's 1847 novel *Jane Eyre* cannot now be read from a twenty-first century perspective without the informing insights of postcolonialism or feminism, then perhaps *Jane Eyre* is also read differently in the light of Jean Rhys's hugely influential appropriation, *Wide Sargasso Sea* (1966).

Parallels to this can be found in the domain of theatrical performance, particularly when charting the influence of the theories and practice of Bertolt Brecht. In his 'Epic theatre' Brecht sought to engage the rational powers of audience response (Willett 1992 [1964]: 33–42). He wanted to break down the empathetic link between spectator and performer partly by means of processes and strategies of 'defamiliarization' or *vefremdungseffekt*, most often translated as 'alienation effect' (Counsell 1996: 102–3; Willett 1992: 91–9). Defamiliarization can be practised as much on a canonical text as on performance practice. Indeed, Brecht's reinterpretations of plays ranging from Shakespeare's *Hamlet* to John Gay's *The Beggars' Opera* are best understood in this context. In *The Resistible Rise of Arturo Ui* (1941), for example, Brecht appropriated Shakespeare's history play *Richard III* to make a very specific point about the rise of fascism in the 1930s. Many appropriations proceed by a similar mechanism of defamiliarization, inviting us as readers or spectators to look anew at a canonical text that we might otherwise have felt we had 'understood' or interpreted to our own satisfaction. In many instances the process of defamiliarization serves to reveal what is repressed or suppressed in an original.

A further theatrical practice that can be examined from the standpoint of appropriation is intercultural performance. According to Patrice Pavis: 'In the strictest sense [intercultural theatre] creates hybrid forms drawing upon a more or less conscious and voluntary mixing of performance traditions traceable to distinct cultural areas' (Pavis 1996: 8). This can mean Western performances which are inflected by the performance techniques and traditions of other cultures, such as British director Peter Brook's Kathakali-influenced version of Indian epic theatre in *The Mahabharata* or French director Ariane Mnouchkine's Japanese Noh and Kabuki inspired versions of Shakespeare's history plays (Kennedy 1993: 279–88); it might also mean Kathakali or Kabuki versions of texts from the Western canon. The problem always in cultural encounters of this kind is that the appropriation can seem hostile or presumptive depending on the direction from which it stems – the question always has to be posed 'who is appropriating who?' and 'on what terms?' Intercultural performance theorists rightly worry over the politics of the transaction taking place, since there is always the danger of an imperialist approach, although some, like Marvin Carlson, would also defend the practice:

> Certain cultural transfers preserve the source culture, the point of view of the other, while it is being absorbed by the receiving culture. Although transformation or re-elaboration of the source material may take place, these are in fact the marks of a truly intercultural representation. A borrowing from another culture is neither a pure and simple citation nor an absolute duplication.
>
> (Pavis 1996: 12)

A whole new set of terms to consider when we are studying adaptation and appropriation, not least in an intercultural context, are mobilized by these reflections: preservation, absorption, re-elaboration, citation, duplication, reception.

Gayatri Chakravorty Spivak has argued that postcolonialism is inherently appropriative in its gestures and its political position-taking: 'in postcoloniality, every metropolitan definition is dislodged. The general mode for the postcolonial is citation, re-inscription, re-routing the historical' (1990: 41). In a parallel move, Sylvie Maurel suggests that 'feminist discourse is to be found in the margins of any construct, of any discursive practice' (1998: 50). Peter Widdowson regards re-visionary writing as 'a crucial component' of the literary, arguing for it as representative of 'a contemporary "counter-culture of the imagination", which in "writing back" to historical texts, and to the historical conjunctures which shaped them, re-writes Authorised History by way of revising its "master-narratives"' (1999: 166). This chapter seeks to examine a cross-section of these 'master-narratives', ranging from Shakespeare's plays, already highlighted in Chapter 3 as central to the history of appropriative art and writing, to seminal novels of the eighteenth, nineteenth, and twentieth centuries. In particular it is interested in the ways in which their appropriations rewrite them from the informing standpoint of some of the most dominant and influential theoretical movements of recent times: feminism, postcolonialism, and queer theory.

JEAN RHYS'S *WIDE SARGASSO SEA*: 'JUST ANOTHER ADAPTATION'?

During an early period of her life when she is housed and schooled in the Dominican Convent of Saint Innocenzia, the protagonist of Jean Rhys's 1966 novel *Wide Sargasso Sea*, Antoinette Mason, reads the lives of the saints. She notices that Innocenzia herself has no story in these compendious volumes: 'We do not know her story, she is not in the book' (Rhys 1987 [1966]: 45). This phrase could serve as epigraph to the entire novel. For what Rhys's novel famously achieves is to provide a marginal character from a canonical work of English literature with a complicated history and a voice. Indeed, Patricia Waugh has suggested that by this action Rhys almost prophetically called into being postmodernism's recurring interest in voicing the silenced or absent characters of the canon: 'prophetically and proleptically she caught what would come to be the dominant literary concerns of the next twenty-five years: the feminist theme of the suppressed "madwoman in the attic"; the structuralist rediscovery of "intertextuality" ...' (1995: 203). Waugh's own intertextual reference here is Sandra Gilbert's and Susan Gubar's seminal work of feminist criticism, *The Madwoman in the Attic* (2000 [1979]). This text, as Waugh suggests, postdates Rhys's novel but encapsulates and extends her interest in the silenced female character of *Jane Eyre*.

The literal (and literary) 'madwoman in the attic' in Rhys's novel is Bertha Rochester, formerly Bertha Antoinette Mason from Jamaica, the first wife of *Jane Eyre*'s complicated sub-Byronic hero Mr Rochester. In Brontë's novel, Bertha is reduced to a mad cackle heard emanating from the upper echelons of Thornfield Hall, Rochester's family estate, and the negative and paranoid constructions of others. Suffering from a hereditary form of insanity, she has been incarcerated by Rochester in an attic room watched over by the servant Grace Poole and concealed from the world. Bertha is marginalized in the text both socially and spatially; Rochester is even prepared to undergo a bigamous marriage to Jane Eyre, although it is during the wedding ceremony itself that the truth of his past is uncovered in public. Rhys's letters in which she deals with the composition of *Wide Sargasso Sea* make it clear that she was anxious to address this marginalization of the part-Creole character of Bertha:

> The Creole in Charlotte Bronte's novel is a lay figure – repulsive, which does not matter, and not once alive, which does. She's necessary to the plot, but always she shrieks, howls and laughs horribly, attacks all and sundry – *off stage*. For me (and for you I hope) she must be right *on stage*.
>
> (Rhys 1985: 156)

Rhys had a personal investment in this approach, being white West Indian and conscious always of being an outsider in the societies in which she lived. In a movement akin to those we have already explored in re-visions of Shakespearean texts, Rhys transports a marginal character from the periphery to the centre; her on-stage, off-stage evocations in the quoted letter are highly suggestive in this respect.

In a method comparable to other literary appropriations that seek to voice silenced or oppressed characters, Rhys achieves her aim of recuperating Antoinette in *Wide Sargasso Sea* by means of first person narration. But instead of according Antoinette the sole perspective in the novel, Rhys interleaves her sections with others articulated by additional voices, in particular that of the novel's 'Rochester' figure, the sanity of whose narrative is ironically unmoored, almost unhinged, by his paranoid response to his situation, both geographical and personal: 'She'll loosen her black hair, and laugh and coax and flatter (a mad girl. She'll not care who she's loving)' (Rhys 1987 [1966]: 135–6). In the crucial final section of the novel, when we are finally transported to England, and quite literally to the terrain of Brontë's text, there is a further unidentified narrative voice which reports an exchange with the servant Grace Poole. The mention of that specific character from Brontë's novel locates the familiar reader for the first time without doubt in the world of *Jane Eyre*, which until this point has been suggested allusively but never firmly identified.

In *Jane Eyre*, of course, Bertha is accorded no voice (except animalistic, lunatic howls, quite literally 'noises off') and little respect in Rochester's damaging and delimited description, which reduces her quite literally to a 'monster' (Brontë 1985 [1847]: 336): 'Bertha Mason is mad; and she came of a mad family; idiots and maniacs through three generations. Her mother, the Creole, was both a madwoman and a drunkard ...' (320). Her entire life-story is reduced to a single chapter (Chapter 27) in *Jane Eyre*. From this minor or marginal plotline, this single chapter, Rhys envisions a whole novel. As Nancy Harrison describes it: 'Rhys structures her novel to show us how a muted text can be revealed to dominate a formerly "dominant" text' (1988: 252). What Rhys also reveals in the rich cultural experience and poetic, even musical, voice she accords Antoinette is the latent racism and prejudice of Brontë's novel and culture. The issue of nomenclature is significant: 'Bertha' is a name imposed on Antoinette by the unnamed male figure who stands for Rochester in the novel, Rochester's *supplement* in Derridean terminology (Derrida 1976: 141–52). This renaming constitutes an attempt to occlude her genetic links with her mother and by extension with the family's supposed hereditary insanity. It also re-enacts what Edward Kamau Brathwaite has described as the process of

'Creolization' in nineteenth-century Jamaica: 'Creolization began with "seasoning" – a period of one to three years, when slaves were branded, given a new name and put under apprenticeship to creolized slaves' (Ashcroft *et al*. 1995: 203).

Helen Carr has described *Wide Sargasso Sea* as 'a ground breaking analysis of the imperialism at the heart of British culture' (1996: 20). Rhys's motivations are simultaneously driven by ethnic and gender implications. She is giving voice to the suppressed stories of the English literary canon, and in this way her novel has become canonical in its own right, a standard bearer for the revisionary impulse in literature, the counter-discourse or counter-culture that Widdowson regards as central to its practice. *Wide Sargasso Sea* represents a central example of both the feminist and the postcolonial novel. It is intriguing, of course, that Rhys 'writes back' to a canonical text by another woman, revealing in the process that for all the liberatory potential Brontë represents in her identity as a published female author, she was in her political attitudes a product of an imperial culture (Spivak 1997 [1989]: 148).

It is only in the very latter stages of Rhys's novel that *Wide Sargasso Sea* quite literally shares space with its literary progenitor. It is in the final section of the novel, which opens with the voice of the unnamed narrator, that a distressed and confused Antoinette is trapped in her attic room in Thornfield Hall. It is as if the novel has been moving towards this moment all along in the reader's imagination, at least that reader who maintains a sense of *Jane Eyre* as an undertow or back-story to *Wide Sargasso Sea*. For it is an inescapable fact that if we read Antoinette's story in the context of Bertha Rochester's we will anticipate her incarceration in the attic, and will expect her eventual death after seeking to burn down Thornfield Hall. Rhys encourages, even nurtures, this expectation by appropriating Brontë's symbolic use of fire throughout *Jane Eyre*. Early on in *Jane Eyre* the young Jane is unjustly locked into a room as punishment by the family with which she is living. Dramatically, she falls unconscious in a state of trauma, awaking to a fire in the room, and has to be rescued. By means of this passage, Brontë establishes a number of the central motifs of her novel, not least incarceration and fire. Rhys repeats that gesture in *Wide Sargasso Sea* when Antoinette's family home is burned down. When in the closing sentences of Rhys's text Antoinette refers to the candle she is holding the alert reader is surely already foreseeing the end of Bertha's life in *Jane Eyre*. Bruce Woodcock suggests that Rhys leaves the ending open to alternatives: 'Rhys's adoption of the present tense and the artistic choice to end the novel at this moment of undefined intent also allow us to imagine Antoinette escaping the pre-determined chain of events into the blank page of the future' (2003: 131). But if the shaping force for interpretation for the majority of *Wide Sargasso Sea*'s readers is *Jane Eyre*, as Rhys surely intended, this seems too utopian in its hopes. In many readers' minds, Antoinette is doomed to repeat the tragic end Brontë envisioned for her.

Wide Sargasso Sea is a novel that is structured around various kinds of repetitions as well as re-visions. Sylvie Maurel, describing the novel as an 'echo-chamber' (1998: 129), writes insightfully of the suggestive title of the text. The Sargasso Sea is famous as a becalmed area amid eddying currents, which as result becomes choked up with a particular species of seaweed. Yet this stagnant locale is also the place to which eels return annually to breed. It encompasses therefore for Maurel both the possibility of stagnant repetition and yet the potential for remarkable creation: 'In its dormant waters, repetition has a creative function; both lethal and fecund, the Sargasso Sea is the seat of cyclical renewal, of creation within repetition' (1998: 129). That same contradictory presence of stifling repetition and the possibility for creating something new drives any work of appropriation, and drives *Wide Sargasso Sea* with a particularly compelling force. It seems an inescapable fact that if, as mentioned, Rhys's novel is structured around repetition and recurring patterns, it is unlikely that either Antoinette or the reader can escape the predetermined fate of her character. When in the novel 'Rochester' makes his drawing of a house, it is, in the reader's mind at least, Thornfield Hall, and Antoinette is already trapped in her attic confine: 'I drew a house surrounded by trees. A large house. I divided the third floor into rooms and in one room I drew a standing woman … ' (Rhys 1987 [1966]: 134). Deep in Antoinette's subconscious, she too seems to foresee this end: 'For I know that house where I will be cold and not belonging, the bed I shall lie in has red curtains and I have slept there many times before, long ago' (92). This is surely the point of characters, stories, and events that are appropriated: their end is predetermined in our imagination via prior knowledge of the precursor text. Antoinette, for all Rhys's investment in according her a voice and history, cannot escape the confines either of her room or her pre-ascribed plot trajectory: 'Now at last I know why I was brought here and what I have to do' (155–6).

Rhys herself seems to have worried about the extent to which her novelistic creation was dependent on *Jane Eyre* for its existence. She genuinely feared that her novel would be regarded as 'just another adaptation' (Rhys 1985: 159) and at one point in her letters she ponders 'unhitching' the novel from its precursor, although she rapidly talks herself out of doing this: 'It might be possible to unhitch the whole thing from Charlotte Brontë's novel, but I don't want to do that. It is that particular Creole I want to write about, not any of the other mad Creoles' (Rhys 1985: 153). Emancipation is a shaping theme in *Wide Sargasso Sea*; the act which promulgated the abolition of slavery in the British colonies is mentioned on the opening page. Yet in tying Antoinette's story so closely to that of Bertha Rochester, Rhys is equally aware that it restricts possibility for her character, preordaining her destiny (Maurel 1998: 133–4). She can liberate Bertha from the attic in the sense that she can award her a voice and a pre-history but she can never entirely emancipate her from the reader's expectations deriving from an awareness of *Jane Eyre*.

Perhaps in the end, that is the only fate we can expect of an appropriative text: just as postcolonialism, by its very designation of being post-, relies on an understanding of the operations of colonialism to derive its full force as a movement, so *Wide Sargasso Sea* is eternally tied to the text it seeks so determinedly to rewrite (Savory 1998: 203). Counter-discourses, in seeking to challenge the values on which a canon is established, cannot help but re-inscribe the canon, but they do so in new, and newly critical, ways. If Walter Benjamin's claim is correct in 'On the Concept of History' (2003a) (also known as 'Theses on the Philosophy of History') that 'There is no document of culture that is not at the same time a document of barbarism. And just as such a document is never free of barbarism, so barbarism taints the manner in which it was transmitted from one hand to another' (Benjamin 2003b: 4.392), then appropriative or revisionary texts such as *Wide Sargasso Sea* are able to reveal or demonstrate what *Jane Eyre*, and by extension nineteenth-century society, suppressed. As Michel Foucault's study of the repressive Victorian discourse on sexuality indicated, the process of revisiting can be a potentially liberatory movement as well as merely recursive (1984 [1978]: 92–102). This is certainly true of the novel we will now move on to discuss, J. M. Coetzee's *Foe*, which, like *Wide Sargasso Sea*, has become canonical in its own right, an exemplar of the counter-discursive move of cultural appropriation.

J. M. COETZEE'S *FOE* AND THE MASTER-TEXT

The origins of parody are ancient. It is a form of imitation usually undertaken for satirical effect or purpose (Dentith 2000). Pastiche is often regarded as a related literary form, since, like parody, it involves imitation, often at the level of style. In its strictest usage, however, in the domains of fine art and music, a 'pastiche' refers more specifically to a medley of references to different styles, texts, or authors. This in turn relates to the previously explored term *bricolage*. If postmodernism is, as we have argued, a complex combination of recreation and fragmentation, then *bricolage* and pastiche would seem to constitute its natural modes of discourse. The question raised by any act of imitation is whether the impersonation is carried out in a mode of celebration or critique. In many cases, however, the truth is a rather more complex hybrid of the two stances.

The recourse to the literary canon in the making of adaptations and appropriations has come to seem almost inevitable in this study in respect that one of the fundamental effects of adaptation is to mobilize a reader's or audience's sense of similarity and difference. It is equally inevitable, then, that the prose narrative that has often been regarded as the foundational text – the originating moment if you like – of the English novel, Daniel Defoe's 1719 *Robinson Crusoe*, should have been the focus of a series of adaptations and reworkings (Watt 1957: 66–103). As well as flattering parallel texts about castaways on desert islands, including *The Swiss Family Robinson*, a number of these reworkings offer a conscious critique of the ideologies and politics of the original. In 1921, Jean Giraudoux published his *Suzanne et le Pacifique*, which, with its female desert island protagonist, immediately took to task the patriarchal and imperialist values of *Robinson Crusoe*. Genette describes this text as a 'refutation' rather than a reworking of Defoe's novel (1997 [1982]: 303). Giraudoux's concern is to expose, in a parallel move to Rhys's treatment of *Jane Eyre* in *Wide Sargasso Sea*, the problematic politics of the original. His novel celebrates the natural fecundity of the island in opposition to the mechanistic impositions of imperial ambition. There are, of course, debates to be had with Giraudoux's unproblematic identification of the female with the natural, and the privileging of the island's naturalness above all else, but it is an approach that was repeated in Michel Tournier's 1967 novel *Vendredi; ou Les Limbes du Pacifique*, which was translated into English in 1984 as *Friday; or The Other Island* (the subtitle is a reference to the novel's French epigraph: '*il y a toujours une autre île*'). As well as indicating the primal instincts that life on the island brings out in Crusoe: 'he returned to the swamp where he had come so near to losing his reason, and stripping off his clothes, let his body sink into the tepid slime' (1984 [1967]: 4), Tournier's sub-Freudian reworking of the novel addresses the sexual needs of his protagonist, which were almost entirely absent from Defoe's text. The island becomes Crusoe's sexual partner, the product of this union being mandrake-like growths across the island, which serve as Tournier's symbol for the transformative effect and impact of colonial activity. This is a third person narrative but one concerned by Crusoe's appropriation of Friday's mind and person in support of his subjection of the island and its flora and fauna to his mastery and control. Friday's point of view is a driving concern in many twentieth-century postcolonial reworkings of Defoe's text, and it is further worth noting that Tournier's text, inflected at all turns as it is by the conventions and discourse of psychoanalysis, is another example of a revisionary work shaped by the theoretical and intellectual interests of its moment of composition.

Gérard Genette's concept of the hypertext which this study has invoked on several occasions might appear to wrest the term away from its more familiar contemporary usage in the idiom of computing where it refers to interconnected texts and graphics on a screen that enable a reader to read across, and cross-refer, documents, but that idea of connection and cross-referral between texts and images remains a potent one in the context of adaptation. One common pattern that emerges from all the texts discussed in this volume is that hypertexts often become 'hyper-hyper-texts', allusive not only to some founding original text or source but also to other known rewritings of that source. Both

Giraudoux's and Tournier's texts seem relevant to one re-vision of the *Robinson Crusoe* narrative that has become canonical in its own right (Attridge 1996: 169), J. M. Coetzee's *Foe* (1986). *Foe*, like *Suzanne et le Pacifique*, is a feminization of *Robinson Crusoe*; indeed, its central character, and for much of the narrative its first person narrator, is called Susan. The intertextual resonance of this is further complicated when we become aware that Susan Barton is the central character in another Defoe novel, *Roxana*, about an eighteenth-century courtesan. These layers of fictional citation and reference are deliberate strategies in this novel which has been usefully described as a 'textual decolonization' by Dominic Head (1997: 14). H. Porter Abbot uses the term 'master-texts' to describe those 'stories that we tell over and over in myriad forms' (2002: 42). A large number of the hypotexts under consideration here are definitive examples of master-texts, especially *Robinson Crusoe* which by being crowned the founding father (and I use the phrase advisedly) of the English novel, has both erased an earlier tradition of women's prose fiction with a romance strain, including the work of Aphra Behn, and enshrined at the head of the English novel tradition a narrative that completely suppresses any role for women.

Coetzee's aim is clearly to undermine the master-text of *Robinson Crusoe*. Its author is known here as 'Foe', playing not only on the sense of enemy or antagonist implicit in that term, but drawing our attention to Defoe's adoption of a writing pseudonym to obscure the class realities of his position: this is a novel concerned at every turn with forgery, fakery, and appropriation in the fictional process. In addition there may be a subtle literary reference to gender in that in early modern literature women were often referred to as 'foemenine' (see, for example, Edmund Spenser's sixteenth-century epic poem *The Faerie Queene*). Since gender is essential to Coetzee's 're-visioning' of Defoe's text this seems highly feasible. This is a novel that constantly offers alternative viewpoints, outcomes, and interpretations, and the plural possibilities of its title are no exception.

In all kinds of ways, literary 'truth' and authenticity are challenged by this metafictional text. The novel opens with a first person perspective that the reader immersed in readings of *Robinson Crusoe* might expect to be that of Crusoe himself: 'At last I could row no further' (Coetzee 1987: 5). The narrative voice turns out, however, to belong to Susan Barton who has been shipwrecked on the hot sands of this particular desert island. The crucial signifier is the 'petticoat' which is all she has escaped with (5). This is, then, a narrative conscious from the start about readerly expectation: 'For readers reared on travellers' tales, the words *desert isle* may conjure up a place of soft sands and shady trees where brooks run to quench the castaway's thirst … But the island on which I was cast away was quite another place' (7). That all-signifying 'But' signals the narrative's decisive turn away from its source text.

We do encounter Cruso in Coetzee's text, although his name is spelt differently on the page (that all important slipped 'e'), and he proves a somewhat different beast compared to the figure in Defoe's text; here he is an old man with a rambling mind and a contradictory memory. Cruso's unreliability as a source of truth is not entirely incompatible with Defoe's text, which is famously full of inconsistencies such as ink running out and Crusoe continuing his journal-writing only moments later. Coetzee's Cruso, however, writes no journal; that act belongs to Susan Barton in another crucial reimagining of the original. And it is a journal that she keeps once she has escaped the island and returned to London. In the course of recreating this journal and the (often unsent) letters that Susan addresses to Foe when she believes he has departed London for Bristol, Coetzee indulges in a virtuoso literary performance, a conscious pastiche or ventriloquism of many of the dominant prose styles of eighteenth-century literature, ranging from the pseudo-authentic journals and 'autobiographies' of Defoe himself to the epistolary ventures of Samuel Richardson. Henry Fielding's fondness for the picaresque road-novel in texts such as *Tom Jones* and *Joseph Andrews* is also evoked in that section of the novel where Susan sets out for Bristol to find Foe, selling his books en route as a very pertinent proof of the material value of literature.

What Coetzee eruditely problematizes here is the vexed question of the ownership of stories. In any feminist argument it would be reasonable to claim that the island story is Susan's, given up to Foe purely to write and publish, although in that act there is an an implicit relinquishing of rights that cannot be ignored. And yet was it ever her story to own? The island experience was a shared one after all, and one which she herself suggests is Cruso's and which she is merely telling in his absence (in this version Cruso dies on the ship journey homeward). The additional question of Friday's rights in the story we will return to. Susan clearly feels a loyalty to the dead Cruso, with whom she had a relationship on the island, but if it is Susan's story or even Cruso's, it is not one she is equipped to tell in the masculine context of the eighteenth-century publishing world: for that she relies on Foe's established reputation. There is, then, a sense in which handing over her story results in a concurrent loss of identity on her part: with no tangible record of her time on the island, she becomes a 'being without substance, a ghost' (Coetzee 1987: 51) unless Foe tells her tale. The authenticating and authorizing processes of literature are clearly being evoked, but so too is the suggestion of (De)Foe as a thief of other people's stories, a plagiarist by any other word. His main profession as a journalist further complicates our understanding of his relationship to the source material for his 'fiction'.

In this subtle and complex way, Coetzee re-animates a centuries-old debate about legal copyright and the ownership of intellectual material. He does so even in the careful punctuation of his novel in printed form: Susan's narratorial statements are encased throughout in quotation marks. This fact emphasizes that the words 'belong' to her, but also problematizes them, rendering the reader painfully aware at all times of the words' retrospective, literary, and therefore constructed nature. The quotation marks are simultaneously a claim to originality and a recognition of artifice. Writing about the legal operation of quotation marks, Margreta de Grazia observes that 'Quotation marks punctuate a page with sanctions – enclosing private materials from public use' (1994: 290), and yet Susan's intention throughout appears to be to make public her experiences on the island.

This reading of Susan's claim to her 'history' ('herstory') as a property or commodity in the public domain is doubly complicated by the layers of internal intertextual reference in Coetzee's text. For, as Dominic Head has acknowledged, Susan is herself a fictional construct, a character from another Defoe novel. One implication is that Foe steals Susan's life story from her to form the base material of another profitable, so-called 'original work of fiction', the 1724 novel, *Roxana*. Another is, however, that he steals from that fictional narrative to give her a false understanding of her own history. Susan seems unable to distinguish truth from fiction by the end. She assumes that the young woman who claims to be her daughter is a fictional creation of Foe's, which of course she is if we as readers choose to invoke the specific intertext of *Roxana*, since in that novel Susan Barton's long-lost daughter returns only to be murdered in a hideously misjudged act of loyalty by Amy the maidservant. But this reading in turn reduces the Susan of *Foe* to purely fictional status. Coetzee's novel appears to toy further with these deconstructive possibilities when, at the close, Susan's first person narration having been replaced by that of an unidentified narrator, destabilizing the narrative further both in temporal and fictional terms, the opening action of slipping overboard is repeated. Narrator and reader travel to the island once more, only to discover, in the ultimate example of narrative slippage, that Susan Barton's corpse is still on the ship. This suggests that the narrative we have just been following was entirely fictitious and without tangible basis, which, when we consider we are reading fiction, is entirely plausible.

Amid all these concerns with Susan Barton's rights or otherwise to the narrative of the island experience, there is another character who shared that experience whose voice is entirely silenced: Friday. As a South African writing in the late twentieth century, Coetzee was all too aware when composing his version of the castaways' story that history is often an imperial narrative in which the voices of those oppressed or vanquished by colonialism are all too frequently silenced: 'In every story there is a silence, some sight concealed, some words unspoken ...' (1987: 141). As Attridge has observed: 'In so far as the oppressed *are* heard [in canonical literature], it is as a marginalised dialect within the dominant language' (1996: 184). The silencing of Friday in this narrative is literal as well as psychological: his tongue has been cut out, possibly, the text intuits, by slavers, possibly by the colonizing Cruso himself. In a reverse move to Jean Rhys's desire to give Bertha Rochester a voice in Antoinette's narrative in *Wide Sargasso Sea*, Coetzee maintains Friday's silence until the close of his novel. As Dominic Head notes, this is both 'a resistance to, yet also the product of, the dominant discourse' (1997: 121). In the strange end section of *Foe*, however, the previously mentioned unnamed and unidentified narrator enters a London property and finds Susan and Foe, presumably dead, in a bed and Friday, in a chilling variation on the trope of the madwoman in the attic, bricked up alive in an alcove. Pressing his ear close to the door, the narrator hears an inexplicable set of noises emanating from behind it: 'From his mouth, without a breath, issue the sounds of the island'

(Coetzee 1987: 154). Friday, still literally silent in vocal terms, becomes or is rendered in his silence a semantic signifier of the island, and all that was suppressed, oppressed, or repressed in Defoe's 'master-text'.

CARYL PHILLIPS'S *THE NATURE OF BLOOD*: INTERWOVEN NARRATIVE AND CIRCULATORY SYSTEMS

We witnessed in Chapter 3 the numerous ways in which adaptations and appropriations of Shakespeare have demonstrated an interest and investment in giving motivation to, voicing, or 'bringing onstage' the victimized, marginalized, or silenced characters of his plays, from Gertrude in *Hamlet* to the entirely unseen Sycorax of *The Tempest*. In turn, texts such as Jane Smiley's *A Thousand Acres* have chosen to accord complex psychological motivation to cardboard cut-out villains such as Goneril and Regan in *King Lear*, in the process transposing Shakespeare's play to the 1970s American Midwest. Caryl Phillips's poetic novel *The Nature of Blood* (1997) does something rather different in that it voices an already central Shakespearean character, Othello, but subjects his narrative and tragic trajectory to re-examination. This is achieved both by means of the multi-perspectival context of juxtaposed first person and third person narratives in the novel, and within the shaping context of analogous stories of diaspora and exile. The novel is structured around the experiences of a sequence of social outsiders, interweaving, and therefore connecting, their tales of persecution on the grounds of ethnicity and religion.

Othello's story is just one of several interleaved narratives in the novel which range across historical and geographical boundaries. Indeed, although the appropriation of Shakespeare's 1604 play can be seen as a guiding creative force in Phillips's text, what we come to recognize as Othello's story does not appear until some one hundred pages in, and the majority of the events in his life that are dealt with in the narrative occur either prior to or during the opening act of Shakespeare's play. Tellingly, in this name-obsessed novel, Othello is never directly named in the text, although the last words of the passages in his narrative voice are 'my name' (1997: 174). If many appropriations actively give voice to certain characters, Phillips seems equally compelled in his narrative to silence the character usually charged with defining and manipulating Othello's actions in the play: Iago, the Ancient is mentioned only once in *The Nature of Blood*, and then only as 'the Ancient' entrusted with the care of the African general's Venetian wife during the sea-journey to Cyprus. The reader is, of course, once again compelled to fill in the gaps with a sense of tragic foreboding and inevitability: we know the future story of this Cypriot encampment and that it will realize something far from the 'happy conclusion' Othello foresees (174).

What we also recognize only too well in the narrative are the lexical signifiers of the twentieth-century Holocaust, such as trains, showers, camps, gas. In his careful interleaving of the early modern Venetian elements of his novel with those scenes set in the concentration camps, Phillips is most concerned with a need to revisit Othello's story in the context of the story of other migrants, outsiders, and refugees. To that end he insists on juxtaposing Othello's story with those of Jewish victims of the twentieth century. He achieves this through strategies of echo and parallel. Stephan Stern, for example, whose narrative begins the novel mid-twentieth century in a Cyprus refugee camp prior to the establishment of the state of Israel, has, like Othello, deserted his wife and child to make a life in a new homeland. Eva Stern's suffering in the Nazi concentration camps is directly paralleled to the execution of Jews in fifteenth-century Venice: the fire and ashes of execution and genocide provide haunting continuities across the centuries.

The Nature of Blood is, then, another veritable echo-chamber of a text; its full emotional and poetic impact is achieved by means of the parallels and analogues found between its variant constituent parts and historical timeframes. We move, in a deliberately unguided if not unstructured way, between fifteenth-century Venice, where members of the Jewish community are wrongly burned at the stake for the supposed murder of a Christian child, the late sixteenth-century Venice which Othello inhabits, and in which we see him visiting the Jewish ghetto of Canareggio by night, the internment camps of Nazi Europe, the postwar refugee camps established in Cyprus (the second Cyprus of the novel echoing in turn the two Venices), and the modern state of Israel. And in the process of all these movements Shakespeare's *Othello* is not the sole informing intertext. The Venetian episodes of the novel suggest and echo the bard's *other* Venetian play about ethnic prejudice *The*

Merchant of Venice, and in the traumatized first person narrative of Eva (Stephan's niece) that canonical text of Holocaust literature, Ann Frank's *Diary*, is clearly evoked. Phillips is offering a troubling version of the old adage that 'History repeats'. One of the most unsettling aspects of the novel is that, having evoked empathy with the persecuted Jews of previous centuries, the narrative closes with a rumination on the inverse prejudice of modern-day Israel in the disenfranchised figure of the Ethopian Jew Malka, who is not even allowed to give blood in her new homeland for fear of polluting 'pure bloodlines'.

The Nature of Blood is intricately structured via a series of repeating images and phrases: blood, fire, smoke, ashes, rivers, food. These words and ideas serve as *leitmotifs*, refrains in the text, and the 'musicality' of this technique has been noted by Bénédicte Ledent (2002: 160). Interestingly the most obvious sources of echo or musical refrain – the lines of Shakespeare's tragic drama – are held at bay for the majority of the novel. Although the events of the 'Othello' passages have obvious connection to those described at the start of Shakespeare's play: 'Her father loved me, oft invited me ...' (1.3.127), 'These things to hear / Would Desdemona seriously incline ...' (1.3.144–5), only some of 'Othello's sentences actively recall famous lines from Phillips's source. 'I possessed only a rudimentary grasp of the language that was being spoken all about me ...' (1997: 108), for example, clearly suggests Othello's claim at 1.3.81, 'Rude am I in my speech', although these words are not directly used until page 181 of the novel and only then in the mouth of a very different character:

> And so you shadow her every move, attend her every whim, like the black Uncle Tom that you are. Fighting the white man's war for him / Wide receiver in the Venetian army / The republic's grinning Satchmo hoisting his sword like a trumpet / You tuck your black skin away beneath their epauletted uniform, appropriate their words (*Rude am I in speech*).

> (1997: 181)

This is one of several moments in the narrative when voices and discourses other than those of the central protagonists are heard. The signifiers here clearly indicate a late twentieth-century voice deriving from the USA – 'wide receiver', 'Satchmo' – and the verse layout both recalls the dramatic verse of Shakespeare's play and evokes the rhythms of contemporary rap, an inherently appropriative form as was suggested in Chapter 2. That the word 'appropriate' figures in this passage also draws attention to Phillips's own fictional methods, as does his inclusion elsewhere of encyclopaedic and dictionary entries on some of his central themes: Venice, ghetto, suicide. These include an entry on *Othello* which emphasizes Shakespeare's own appropriation of an Italian source, a short story by Cinthio, when manufacturing his remarkable play.

In *The Nature of Blood*, an individual's narrative often commences at a supposed endpoint or terminus of their story (Eva's liberation from the camp for example), only to then move backwards in time. The interlocking and repeating circular movements of the narrative leave the question open as to whether Phillips's vision is hopeful or despairing at the end. Malka's story would seem to imply that history is simply a repeating series of tragedies and cruelties. The novel closes, after all, with the image of an impossible embrace. In the end, however, perhaps the real answer lies in the image of circularity. There can be no easy answers and no closure on such complicated themes. In this subtle examination of memory and forgetting, the reader cannot shut out knowledge of certain facts. Just as Eva's story cannot, and does not, end at the point of liberation from the camp – we, as readers, are forced to witness her painful efforts to survive after the war, resulting in her failed trip to England and her eventual suicide – so we know that Othello's story does not cease at that moment of happy arrival on the shores of Cyprus. Phillips's allusive frames force us to read on further, beyond these pages, and the tragic impetus of his novel proves inescapable as a result.

MICHAEL CUNNINGHAM'S *THE HOURS*: RIFFING ON *MRS DALLOWAY*

Michael Cunningham has described his 1998 novel *The Hours*, a novel told via a triptych of female voices stretching from early twentieth-century England through 1940s Los Angeles to 1990s New York, as a 'riff' on Virginia Woolf's *Mrs Dalloway* (Young 2003: 31). Woolf's 1925 novel tells the story of a group of Londoners on a single day in June

1923. Cunningham never directly retells or rewrites these events and yet their presence is everywhere felt in *The Hours*. Indeed, 'The Hours' was Woolf's working title for her effort to develop and extend her short story 'Mrs Dalloway in Bond Street' into novel-length form (her diary entry for 30 August 1923 is used as an epigraph to *The Hours* [Woolf 1981: 263]). At various stages in Cunningham's narrative we witness Virginia Woolf thinking her experimental novel into being; we also see a 1949 US housewife, Laura Brown, escaping from the quotidian *ennui* of her life by reading the novel; and in the 1990s sections, the implicit connection between Clarissa Vaughan and her novelistic counterpart is made explicit: Richard, Clarissa's friend and a writer, jokingly calls her 'Mrs Dalloway', forcing Clarissa to reflect: 'There was the matter of her existing first name, a sign too obvious to ignore ...' (Cunningham 1998: 10–11). Cunningham enjoys the postmodern joke here; his inter-textual pastiche is full of signs and signifiers, some of which are too obvious to ignore, of its relationship to its literary precursor. Other names are equally telling: Laura Brown's deliberately invokes the char-acter in Woolf's influential essay 'Mr Bennett and Mrs Brown', which constituted, in part, a manifesto for a new approach to fiction and which differentiated her own writing from that of Arnold Bennett, H. G. Wells, and John Galsworthy among others (1988 [1923]).

Cunningham's musical analogy of the 'riff', one we have already invoked in this volume on frequent occasions as an informing analogue to the process of adaptation and appropriation, is insightful. As Tory Young notes: 'In its suggestion of a known melody reverberating throughout a new score, this musical definition is more compelling than some of the literary terminology – "imitation", "homage" – that critics have used to describe it' (2003: 33). The specific analogy of 'riff' with the approaches to adaptation adopted by jazz music – 'riff' in the *Oxford English Dictionary* definition is 'a short repeated phrase in jazz' – is worth pausing to reflect on. Throughout his career, Terence Hawkes has drawn a suggestive parallel between persistent interpretations and rein-terpretations of Shakespeare in Western culture and the improvisational techniques of jazz (see, for example, Hawkes 1992). Cunningham here riffs not solely on a single sourcetext, although *Mrs Dalloway* is clearly the crucial intertext for his novel, but creates a work that exists in sym-biotic interplay with Woolf's fiction and non-fiction (letters, essays, diaries), and her personal biography. Cunningham has frequently acknowledged his debt to Hermione Lee's 1996 biography of Woolf. That symbiotic interplay occurs at the level of form as well as plot. The prose style of *The Hours* consciously imitates Woolf's stream-of-consciousness technique, echoing resonant words and phrases from *Mrs Dalloway* such as 'plunge' (Woolf 1992 [1925]: 3; Cunningham 1998: 9). The echoes are not restricted to *Mrs Dalloway*, but extend to other works in Woolf's *oeuvre* as Cunningham lovingly pastiches her writing style and aesthetic.

Events in *The Hours*, are, however, persistently shaded and shadowed by those in *Mrs Dalloway*: Septimus Smith's suicide in a leap on to the London railings as he is pursued by doctors, whom he regards as unsympathetic to his 'shell-shock' or post-traumatic stress disorder, is reworked in Richard's suicidal leap from his New York apartment. Richard chooses to end his life because he is in the late stages of the AIDs virus. Cunningham's personal sexual politics, as well as his obvious feminist sympathies, inform his particular appropriation of *Mrs Dalloway*. This is an appropriation informed as much by late twentieth-century queer politics and theory as it is by its feminist and postmodern counterparts. Cunningham's particular 'movement of proximation' finds a late twentieth-century equivalent to the warfare which shaped its first half to be virulent pandemics such as AIDs. In this respect his reworking of the themes of *Mrs Dalloway* in a modern context might be felt to be wholly tragic in tone. But there is also a liberatory treatment of gay rights and politics at the heart of this novel. Cunningham achieves for his characters a freedom of relationships beyond the heterosexually prescribed 'norm' which was well beyond the reach of Woolf's own circumscribed community for all Bloomsbury's sexual experimentation. In Cunningham's version, Clarissa does not marry Richard, who is openly gay, but is instead coupled in a rich and rewarding relationship with Sally Seton; this relationship was only hinted at on a subterranean level in *Mrs Dalloway* although it, of course, in turn reworked the intimate friendship between Woolf and Vita Sackville-West.

The triple timeline of Cunningham's novel helps the reader to register the seismic social shifts that have taken place since Woolf was writing: the tense and contained kitchen kiss between Laura Brown and her neighbour Kitty serves as an indication of the containment of female sexual and social possibility in 1949, but in the 1990s sections of the novel the full potential for diverse relationships and friendships is realized. Cunningham updates Woolf's novel in successive movements through his triptych of characters in the temporal, geographical, and cultural manner which we have already identified as a common factor to these 'movements of proximation' (Genette 1997 [1982]: 304). London in the 1920s is replaced in succession by 1949 Los Angeles and 1990s New York. *Mrs Dalloway*'s spatial location of Westminster is substituted and supplemented by NY's West Village, itself a famous historical locale in gay consciousness as the site of the 1960s Stonewall Riots. This is a novel that builds into its music and movements the translocations and transpositions that are a factor of appropriative literature. It should, however, be stressed that no one place completely replaces another; each element of the triptych contains within it links and connections to the rest. This is made most obvious in the closing moments of the novel when, following Richard's suicide, his estranged mother arrives at Clarissa's apartment. Belatedly readers realize that this Toronto librarian, whose absence from his life obsessed Richard and coloured his own authorial productions, is actually Laura Brown from the LA segments of the novel. Similarly, a novel that starts with Woolf's own 1940 suicide by drowning comes full circle by the close with Richard's leap to his death in emulation of one of her literary creations.

Circular and repeating movements are a vital aspect of this novel's aesthetic structure. This is a mode we have already seen in operation in other appropriations in this chapter, from Rhys's repetition-soaked *Wide Sargasso Sea*, the repeating events in revised circumstances of Phillips's *The Nature of Blood*, and the narratorial slippage in Coetzee's *Foe*. As well as these web-like connections between the three voices and settings of *The Hours*, there are numerous linking and repeated symbols of the circular and the spherical, which form a verbal *leitmotif* in the narrative: cups, bowls, cakes (Young 2003: 31). In Stephen Daldry's 2002 film version this imagery was repeated once again, this time in a visual context and medium, but the true connective tissue was provided by Philip Glass's remarkable river-like, undulating, piano-based soundtrack.

Part of the novel's music is temporal as well as spatial. Linear sequence is deliberately denied in *The Hours*. We begin with Woolf's ending as it were, her river suicide, but then we revert to a time in her life before *Mrs Dalloway* has even been written. These movements backwards as well as forwards are crucial to the anti-linear structure of Phillips's history-driven *The Nature of Blood* as well. It has become something of a commonplace to associate the circular and anti-linear narrative with women's writing (Sanders 2001: 142); Cunningham once again associates his personal perspective as a gay writer here with a methodology that has been socially (and critically) gendered as female but which he here reclaims for another readership and community. The repetition and circular sweeps are also perhaps inevitable in a novel that looks back to a canonical source and embeds within its own pages the textual traces of Woolf's remarkable and musical creation. As Clarissa Vaughan observes stepping out into the streetscape of 1990s New York on her own urban walking experience, at seventy years remove from her British namesake who commenced Woolf's novel with this action in 1920s London: 'There are still the flowers to buy' (Cunningham 1998: 9).

7

'WE "OTHER VICTORIANS" '; OR, RETHINKING THE NINETEENTH CENTURY

What becomes evident from any historicized consideration of appropriation is that interest invariably clusters around certain authors and texts: Shakespeare, mythology, and fairy tale have all been advanced in this volume as archetypal texts, ripe for appropriation and re-vision. The interest in specific texts, such as Defoe's *Robinson Crusoe* or Brontë's *Jane Eyre*, has also in part been explained in terms of the canon. As Chantal Zabus eloquently observes: 'Each century has its own interpellative dream-text: *The Tempest* for the seventeenth century; *Robinson Crusoe* for the eighteenth century; *Jane Eyre* for the nineteenth century; *Heart of Darkness* for the turn of the twentieth century. Such texts serve as pre-texts to others and underwrite them' (2002: 1). Defoe's novel carries the specific burden of signification as an early experiment in the form; *Jane Eyre* is a signifying text for feminism, as well as an intriguing dalliance with popular subgenres such as the Gothic romance. Canonicity, it has been posited, is almost a required feature of the raw material for adaptation and appropriation. If the implied pleasure involved in the action of assessing the similarities and differences between texts, between source and imitation, which we have elsewhere argued for as fundamental to the reading and spectating experience of adaptation, is to be possible it requires prior knowledge of the text(s) being assimilated, absorbed, reworked, and refashioned by the adaptive process.

What, however, also emerges from any historical exploration of appropriation is that it is not only specific texts or authors who elicit the kind of ongoing, evolving interest that stimulates the adaptive process, but in certain respects it is specific genres, or even specific genres as they emerge during a particular time-period, which become the focus of a shared (re)creative impulse. A particular and sustained example of this is undoubtedly the Victorian era (1837–1901). As this chapter will indicate, appropriations return again and again to the scene of the mid-nineteenth century for characters, plotlines, generic conventions, and narrative idiom and style. What we need to examine therefore are the motives behind this interest. It is fair to say that the Victorian era had its own investment in adaptation. Adrian Poole has written of the predominance of Shakespeare in the artistic productions of the Victorian era, from plays to poetry to painting to fiction (2004). George Eliot, Thomas Hardy, Charles Dickens, and the Pre-Raphaelite painters all alluded to the Bard. And it was not only the writers of previous eras who were subject to the recreative impulses of the Victorians: Dickens's novels and characters, as well as those of Sir Walter Scott, enjoyed a vivid afterlife on the public stages of the day. Dickens even satirized this fact in *Nicholas Nickleby*, where Nicholas encounters a 'literary gentleman' who 'had dramatized in his time two-hundred-and-forty-seven novels as fast as they had come out – and some of them faster than they had come out' (cited in Cox 2000: 136). John Fowles makes similar comic capital in his own postmodern recreation of the Victorian novel, *The French Lieutenant's Woman*, when the servant Sam Farrow is compared to Sam Weller from *Pickwick Papers*, a character who we learn he knows not from Dickens's novel but rather from its populist stage adaptation (Fowles 1996 [1969]: 46). Dickens's objections to the quality of some of the dramatic adaptations of his work are a further indication of marked distinctions between the productions of so-called 'high' and 'low' culture in the period. High art was invested with the values of authorship and originality; popular culture with the belatedness of adaptation. In the twentieth century, with the advent of the newly inaugurated discipline of Cultural Studies, scholars such as Stuart Hall and Raymond Williams saw rather more cause for celebrating the adaptive tendencies of popular cultural forms (Hall 1972: 96). It is worth adding that the Victorian era appealed as a subject to the revisionary era of cultural studies partly because of the lively interaction and cross-fertilization between the high and low arts in this period.

The genre which most obviously bridged the threshold between high and low, élite and popular, in the nineteenth century was the novel (see Wheeler 1994). Many novels were published in instalments, encouraging readerly addiction to plotlines and characters, and honing the authorial skills of creating suspense by means of the 'cliffhanger' ending that still influences contemporary soap opera on radio and television. It is, therefore, no coincidence that the generic mode in the Victorian era most constantly looked to by adaptors and appropriators is prose fiction. But it is not simply the genre of the novel *per se* that proves a rich seam for contemporary adaptation to mine. The nineteenth century also witnessed a proliferation of sub-genres within the novel form: there were early experiments with suspense fiction, encouraged by the tendency to publish in instalments; sensation literature, which found its own provenance in a contemporary predilection for scandalous legal trials and which had a markedly feminocentric character, reached its peak in the 1860s; detective fiction began to emerge as a genuine sub-genre in its own right, related as it was to a wider interest in crime, criminology, and forensic science in the Victorian novel; and there were developments such as the industrial and the provincial novel, as pioneered by Elizabeth Gaskell, Thomas Hardy, and George Eliot among others.

In the late twentieth century, as the postmodernist movement developed its own interest in metafiction and writing which acknowledged its sources in a more explicit and deconstructive mode than previously, the Victorian era offered a diverse range of genres and methodologies to examine and appropriate. Dominic Head identifies this impulse in Graham Swift's *Waterland*, for example: 'Part of Swift's self-consciousness is to make use of a number of fictional genres identified with English fiction in the nineteenth century: the dynastic saga, the gothic novel, the detective story, and, most important, the provincial novel in which character is closely linked with environment' (Head 2002: 205). Head stresses that the result of Swift's reworkings is not parody *per se* but rather a process of reinvigoration achieved via modern and postmodern inflection (205). The impulse is towards quotation and recreation but less with the deconstructive purpose of satire in mind than the postmodern effect of innovation through fragmentation. A similar case has already been made for Baz Luhrmann's consciously postmodern approach to cultural intertexts in films such as *Moulin Rouge* (see

Chapter 4) and J. M. Coetzee's approach to eighteenth-century literary style in his novel *Foe* (see Chapter 6).

Many of the best-known modern 'recreations' of the Victorian novel self-consciously position themselves in relation to the populist subgenres of the nineteenth century. It is an act of recreation, however, that entails critique and re-evaluation as much as it does stylistic mimicry or pastiche. John Fowles's *The French Lieutenant's Woman* is a romance that also carries traces of the mystery novel and the scientific tract within its pages; A. S. Byatt's *Possession*, a self-conscious reworking of the act of literary criticism as a form of detective fiction – 'Literary critics make natural detectives' (1991: 237) – signals in its subtitle, *A Romance*, a link to the romance genre so evident in the paintings of the Pre-Raphaelites. These novels may not appropriate a specific writer or text, but they constitute an appropriation in the terms established here since they seek to recreate and refashion a particular literary genre, period, and style. To quote Graham Allen on this form of 'transtextuality': 'Novels may signpost their architextual relation to certain genres, sub-genres or conventions by including a subtitle, as in Ann Radcliffe's Gothic novel *The Mysteries of Udolpho: A Romance* ...' (2000: 102). Byatt's subtitle may even be a direct echo of Radcliffe's. Certainly, both Fowles's and Byatt's texts are laid out on the page in a manner reminiscent of much nineteenth-century fiction, not least the novels of Eliot and Hardy, with copious literary quotations providing the shaping epigraphs to individual chapters. In this respect they materially as well as aesthetically re-create the mode of the Victorian novel with all its paratextual material.

In the case of *The French Lieutenant's Woman*, these quotations derive from actual and identified nineteenth-century sources, but also from 'historical' recreations such as the work of Asa Briggs and G. M. Young. There is an interesting recognition implicit in this of the textuality of history and of history's status as text or narrative. In *Metahistory*, Hayden White famously argued that any work of history was as much a piece of rhetorical construction as any work of fiction and that the play of rhetorical surfaces across historical narrative influenced the reader as much as the events or 'facts' being recounted (1973: 3). History, in this account, is a matter of perspective; it is influenced and shaped by the agenda or subject-position of the historian. Several of the adaptations we are considering here that revisit the nineteenth century or seek to voice marginalized or repressed groups suggest something similar in their search to reveal 'hidden histories', the stories between the lines of the published works of fact and fiction. Metafiction and metahistory collide in interesting and provocative ways in the course of this self-consciousness about the constructed nature of texts.

In A. S. Byatt's *Possession* the chapter epigraphs she provides stand at one stage further removed from the period she is appropriating since they are authorial creations that merely resemble 'real' literature from the nineteenth century. In (re)creating the verse of her Victorian poets Randolph Ash and Christabel LaMotte – the subjects of the academic research of her modern counterpart characters Roland Michell and Maud Bailey – Byatt alludes to the work of actual nineteenth-century poets such as Robert Browning, Christina Rossetti, and Emily Dickinson. Ash's work offers a particular parallel with Browning who was admired for a kind of poetic ventriloquism in his work, his ability to create and re-create individual voices, real and fictional, in his dramatic monologues. Indeed, the biography of Ash written by one of the novel's characters, Mortimer Cropper, is entitled *The Great Ventriloquist* as if to draw attention to this mode within Byatt's own writing (Hulbert 1993: 56) which in the course of this novel pastiches letters, journals, and poetry from the Victorian era, as well as the tone and idiom of feminist and postmodern literary criticism. A similar method is on display in John Fowles's 1977 novel *A Maggot* which recounts the events leading up to the birth of Ann Lee, founder of the Shaker movement. Although in many respects the narrative of *A Maggot* is a meticulous reconstruction of a historical moment and idiom, the novel's title alerts us to the fact that this is not pure, unadulterated, historical reconstruction. In eighteenth-century terminology a 'maggot' was a whim or a caprice: the caprice is entirely Fowles's own, since he interrupts the course of the narrative at various stages to remind the reader that, despite appearances to the contrary, the novel is an artfully constructed version of events (Connor 1996: 146).

These 'recreational' fictions are never pure ventriloquism, then. They rely on their readers' awareness that they are reading from the vantage point of the modern era. Byatt ensures this deliberate disjuncture by interweaving dual storylines and parallel romances in the nineteenth and twentieth centuries. Fowles goes even further by building into his postmodern narratives a metafictional awareness of the modern idiom and understanding inflecting his, and our, responses to his historical characters and themes. Phrases in *The French Lieutenant's Woman* such as 'We meet here, once again, this bone of contention between the two centuries ...' (1996 [1969]: 52) draw attention to the encounter between the mindsets of the two periods, as does the encounter between the author and his character in a railway carriage in one notorious chapter of the novel. Fowles's mode of recreation is one that resists wholesale ventriloquism of the Victorian narrative style, depending instead on the telling role of juxtaposition, comparison, and contrast that we have already seen as a driving force of the appropriative mode. He asserts, for example, that he is not the omniscient narrator so memorable from the majority of nineteenth-century fiction: 'If I have pretended until now to know my characters' minds and innermost thoughts, it is because I am writing in (just as I have assumed some of the vocabulary and "voice" of) a convention universally accepted at the time of my story: that the novelist stands next to God' (97). His is by contrast the era of the 1960s and poststructuralism: 'I live in the age of Alain Robbe-Grillet and Roland Barthes ...' (97). In Chapter 13 of *The French Lieutenant's Woman*, Fowles's God proves to be an existentialist creation. This represents not so much a deconstruction of authorship as an overt refusal of it and as such offers an intriguing echo of Barthes's arguments for the 'freedom' of the reader in his theoretical writings, although in Fowles that freedom is reimagined as a freedom of the novelistic character.

James Wilson's *The Dark Clue*, while less explicit about the metafictional aspect of its appropriation of the Victorian mode of fiction writing, nevertheless achieves something very similar to Fowles's and Byatt's fictions, by pastiching the style of nineteenth-century sensation fiction, a mode which reached its peak in the 1860s (Pykett 1994: 1). Wilson recreates sensation fiction's meticulous reconstructions of quasi-legalistic eye-witness statements in its first person narratives, while also alluding to a specific canonical text: Wilkie Collins's 1860 novel *The Woman in White*. *The Woman in White* is famous not only as the progenitor of this mode of sensation fiction but also as the precursor of crime fiction as a genre, and the specific mode of the detective novel which Collins would realize in a fuller incarnation in his later text, *The Moonstone* (1868). Again, Wilson signals his interest in the revisiting of the

Victorian subgenres of the mystery and the crime novel in his subtitle to *The Dark Clue*, 'A novel of suspense', and in his expert pastiching of Collins's own predilection for a narrative constructed via a combination of letters, journal entries, and legal testimonies. Lyn Pykett has indicated just how much Collins's novel owed to the popular stage melodramas of his day (1994: 4) and Wilson seems to acknowledge this via his inclusion of a pastiche of a play at one point in the narrative.

Such was *The Woman in White*'s significance in its own era that there were multiple stage adaptations and even tie-in merchandise (Collins 1999 [1860]: vii); this cultural potency continues into the present era when it is the subject of musical and television adaptation, once again acknowledging the novel's creative proximity to melodrama as a form. Wilson's novel meanwhile reanimates and re-voices two of the protagonists from *The Woman in White*: Walter Hartright the painter, and his sister-in-law Marian Halcombe. Between them this incongruous pair solved the original mystery of Collins's novel, which is concerned with the feigned demise of Marion's sister Laura, who has in truth been placed in an asylum under a false identity by her villainous husband Sir Percival Glyde. Here Walter and Marion serve once again as amateur sleuths. This time, however, their assigned task is to research the life of the late painter J. M. W. Turner, about whom Hartright has been commissioned to write a biography. In a parallel mode to that of Byatt and Fowles in their 'recreations', Wilson here merges fictional and real figures from the Victorian era. What he is also able to do in the process is to make explicit many of the sexual tensions which are only implicit in Collins's text but which have been recognized and discussed by generations of readers and critics. John Sutherland has located the sexual undertow of *The Woman in White* in the face-off between Marian and Count Fosco, the melodramatic Italian villain of the piece, but there is surely also sexual chemistry between Walter and Marian, despite his surface passion for, and indeed ultimate marriage to, her more conventionally beautiful half-sister. Wilson seems almost to satisfy readerly expectation in this respect when a troubled sexual encounter takes place between his protagonists late in the novel.

This sexually aggressive element in the text of *The Dark Clue* is part of the novel's wider investment in exploring the sexual undercurrents and repressions of the Victorian era. This constitutes much of the hidden mystery of Turner's life that Walter uncovers in the course of his biographical research – in a move parallel to that of Byatt's *Possession*, the art of the biographer is here paralleled with that of the detective or the forensic scientist – and which he has to confront as a darker element of his own personality in the course of the narrative. In this respect it should be stressed that Wilson seems keen to darken and complicate Collins's rather perfect and good hero, the aptly named 'Hartright'. One of the aspects of Turner's painterly technique that begins to fascinate and obsess Hartright (and again, as in Byatt's novel, the researcher becomes at several turns possessed and haunted by his subject) is his deployment of *chiaroscuro* in his work. The *Oxford English Dictionary* offers a triple definition of this term. In painting terminology it is 'the treatment of light and shade in drawing and painting'. This is a recognizable element of Turner's technique and one that Hartright seeks to emulate: the novel encourages an awareness of Turner's paintings throughout in order to understand how and why events unfold as they do. But *chiaroscuro* can also mean 'the use of contrast in literature', a driving force as we have seen of appropriation. And additional it refers, via its Italian etymology, to the 'half-revealed' (*chiaro* = clear; *oscuro* = dark/obscured); Wilson's title *The Dark Clue* is a transliteration of *chiaroscuro* in some respects, but it highlights the investment of detective fiction in revealing the initially obscured, in bringing things to light that were in shade, the same idea that Graham Swift's novel *The Light of Day* was seen to pun so vibrantly on in Chapter 2. Possibly a parallel to the biographer's art is being suggested in the phrase, although it also draws attention to the novel's uncomfortable revelation of the dark secrets of Victorian society, a world of prostitution and pornography that drags Walter quite literally into its back alleys. This is the same undercurrent to Victorian society that troubles and concerns Fowles in *The French Lieutenant's Woman*. The dual perspective highlighted as a dominant mode in Fowles's novel instructs us as readers to see the discrepancies and contradictions inherent in our understanding of Victorian society: 'What are we faced with in the nineteenth century? An age where woman was sacred; and where you could buy a thirteen-year-old girl for a few pounds ... Where more churches were built than in the whole previous history of the country; and where one in sixty houses in London was a brothel ...' (1996 [1969]: 258). The reader is acting as a detective of sorts when encountering this fiction, recognizing the parallels but also the significant differences between the rendition of the nineteenth century achieved in the novels and their current context, and deciphering a whole set of codes and clues into the process.

The Victorian era and its active underworld would seem to offer a very specific example of these kinds of social and cultural contradictions and this may in part explain the ongoing fascination with appropriating the modes of nineteenth-century fiction more generally in contemporary writing. There are also parallels with our own largely urban era that should not be underestimated. In the novels of Dickens and Collins, among many others, London functions as a virtual character. The Victorian era throws into relief some of our own more contemporary concerns with class and social hierarchy and with questions of empire and imperialism. As Gayatri Chakravorty Spivak has noted, 'It should not be possible to read nineteenth-century British literature without remembering that imperialism, understood as England's social mission, was a crucial part of the cultural representation of England to the English' (1997 [1989]: 148). All of these are reasons for the ongoing interest in offering knowing renditions and reworkings of the concerns of Victorian fiction.

But it is worth homing in even further on this interest. For as well as the Victorian era in its totality, a particular interest in the decade of the 1860s has emerged. This was the decade, as we have already seen, of sensation fiction and the emergence of related subgenres such as the detective novel and the murder mystery. *Possession*, *The Dark Clue*, and *The French Lieutenant's Woman* are all partly set in the 1860s. As well as Collins's *The Woman in White* and *The Moonstone*, Charles Dickens's *Great Expectations*, though its action was set some years earlier, was published in the 1860s. We will consider this novel in further detail later, but suffice to say here that it bears marked traces of the contemporary interest in crime and the modes and techniques of suspense fiction; Wemmick's library of studies of criminology and convict literature is just one obvious marker of this fact in the novel. But, as that novel's acknowledged and highly developed interest in theories of nature and nurture suggests (Dickens 1994 [1861]: xiv), the 1860s represent a decisive turn in terms of postmodern rethinkings of the Victorian novel and its deeper context of Victorian social and cultural values. For this was the era that witnessed one of the greatest ever challenges to religious understandings of the world and of identity, in the shape of Charles Darwin's theory of evolution. *The Origin of the Species* was first published in 1859. It is no coincidence that John Fowles furnishes many of the chapter epigraphs in *The French Lieutenant's Woman* from Darwin's influential ideas of adaptation and environment, or that his central male character is a geologist, a scientist open to the Darwinian approach to understanding the world around him.

Great Expectations was first published in instalment form between December 1860 and August 1861 in the periodical *All the Year Round*. In 1860, this periodical had also published two significant extrapolations in essay-form of Darwin's theory of adaptation, variation, and survival: 'Species', published in June, and 'Natural Selection', published in July. The influence of this on Dickens's novel, which argues, via the plot trajectories of both Pip and Estella, that biological origins are only ever one part of our complex social and environmental make-up, cannot be underestimated. In *Darwin's Plots* Gillian Beer has argued that Darwin's prose was informed by his reading across several disciplines and that he found the literary figure of analogy especially helpful for articulating his scientific ideas (1983: 80). It seems equally apposite that novels engaged in the process of literary adaptation, in creating analogues and variants of their own according to cultural, geographical, and historical context, should be drawn to Darwinian theories.

So the Victorian era proves in the end ripe for appropriation because it throws into sharp relief many of the overriding concerns of the postmodern era: questions of identity; of environmental and genetic conditioning; repressed and oppressed modes of sexuality; criminality and violence; the urban phenomenon; the operations of law and authority; science and religion; the postcolonial legacies of the empire. In the rewriting of the omniscient narrator of nineteenth-century fiction, often substituting for him/her the unreliable narrator we have recognized as common to appropriative fiction, postmodern authors find a useful metafictional method for reflecting on their own creative authorial impulses. This chapter will conclude therefore with a close reading of one particular contemporary novel that embodies all of these impulses in its remarkable appropriation and adaptation of Charles Dickens's *Great Expectations*, and which therefore serves as a valuable test case for the claims made above: Peter Carey's *Jack Maggs* (1997).

COMING OUT OF THE SHADOWS: PETER CAREY'S
JACK MAGGS

Like so many of the writers explored and invoked in these pages, Australian novelist Peter Carey's interest in appropriation is not limited to a single work in his *oeuvre*. In a manner akin to J. M. Coetzee or John Fowles, he has long been recognized as a deeply intertextual writer. Novels such as *Illywhacker* (1985) and *Oscar and Lucinda* (1988) have been linked to nineteenth-century writing, in particular the work of Charles Dickens, South American texts of magic realism, and the films of Werner Herzog, to name a few (Woodcock 2003: 82). The remarkable opening sequence of *Oscar and Lucinda* which depicts Oscar's upbringing among the Plymouth brethren and its episode of the forbidden plum pudding owes much to Edmund Gosse's work of retrospective Victorian autobiography, *Father and Son* (1907). Possibly in an act of deliberate disingenuousness, Carey denied at the time of *Oscar and Lucinda* that he was well-read in Dickens (Woodcock 2003: 58) but there could be no doubt of his immersion in the works of the Victorian novelist by the time of his 1997 novel *Jack Maggs* which is a direct appropriation of *Great Expectations*. The 'Jack Maggs' of Carey's title is his postcolonial reworking of Dickens's convict Abel Magwitch, the man whose New South Wales fortune is deployed in fashioning Pip Pirrip as a gentleman of 'great expectations' in that novel. If Dickens's novel is, as Kate Flint has described it, a text imbued with the motif of return or, at least, of trying to return (Dickens 1994 [1861]: vii), then Carey's fiction is doubly so. He returns to the story of Magwitch and the return of Magwitch to London to meet with his 'adopted son' Pip, here transformed into the rather more reprehensible figure of Henry Phipps, imposing on it a distinctly postcolonial set of political values and concerns. As with Jean Rhys's exposure of the implicit imperialism of *Jane Eyre* in *Wide Sargasso Sea*, Bruce Woodcock suggests that Carey exposes the repressions and prejudices at the base of Dickens's text and Victorian culture:

> *Jack Maggs* juxtaposes the hidden and the visible to reveal a terrible social violence beneath the surface of the imperial ideal … [It] is Peter Carey's *Wide Sargasso Sea*: an act of postcolonial retaliation against a parent culture. Like Jean Rhys's novel, it rewrites elements of a canonical text from the heart of the English literary tradition to

reveal the hidden alternative history that cultural hegemony has effaced or suppressed.

(2003: 120)

If Dickens's novel views Abel Magwitch almost entirely through Pip's eyes and layered first person narration, Carey inverts the perspective so that we see events very much from Maggs's point of view. We start the novel at the point of Maggs's return from the penal colony of New South Wales. Carey quite literally effects for him a conditional pardon within the context of his novel. As well as the obvious Dickensian hypotext, Carey is reworking the genre of Australian convict literature, a prime example of which would be Marcus Clarke's *His Natural Life* (1885). Thomas Keneally's *The Playmaker*, discussed in Chapter 2, works within a similar textual framework. Both Carey and Keneally write from a self-consciously postcolonial vantage point, 'writing back' to the question of convict transportation and the creation of the British penal settlement in Australia. For Keneally this has the further resonance of the damage it wrought on the indigenous aboriginal communities.

Influential on Carey's response to issues of empire in Australian culture was Robert Hughes's book *The Fatal Shore*, published in 1988, which directly discusses *Great Expectations* in the postcolonial context. In turn, and in a passage that cites Carey as a postcolonial author, Edward Said picked up on this study in the Introduction to *Culture and Imperialism* (1993: xvi–xvii), further evidence were it needed of the influence of theory on appropriations. Said suggested that in *Great Expectations* the transported convict Magwitch serves as a metaphor for the relationship between England and its colonial offspring: 'The prohibition placed on Magwitch's return is not only penal but imperial: subjects can be taken to places like Australia, but they cannot be allowed a "return" to metropolitan space, which, as all Dickens's fiction testifies, is meticulously charted, spoken for ...' (xvii). Carey allows Magwitch that return in the context of a novel which, like so many of the adaptations of nineteenth-century fiction discussed in this chapter, evinces a deep fascination with the metropolitan space of London.

In *Jack Maggs*, Carey rewrites the conventional convict's ending as well as Magwitch's specific fate in Dickens's novel, where he dies in Pip's arms. Carey allows Maggs an additional 'return' to his Australian 'home' and family. This proves a more complex rewriting than first appearances might suggest, since throughout the narrative Maggs persistently denies his Australian identity, rejecting his family there in favour of an obsessive interest with the aborted child in his criminal past and the 'adopted' Phipps. Máire ní Fhlathúin indicates the ways in which the novel, imitating the generic conventions of 1860s sensation fiction, repeats tropes of failed parentage, not least via the figure of the dying William IV; the novel opens in 1837 with an ailing king and the accession of Queen Victoria imminent. She argues that Carey does not entirely escape the paradigms he seeks to expose since he merely replaces an idealized Australian patriarchy for the imperial version the novel critiques. The final image that readers are given of Magwitch on his return to New South Wales is one of imperial re-creation both within the family and at the local cricket club (1999: 90). The limits to Carey's postcolonial perspective are, perhaps, revealed by this, as well as by the ostensible absence of the aboriginal voice from this text, although in the extended debates about property and ownership in the novel many of the legal discourses of the Australian land rights debate are self-consciously recalled.

Carey's approach to Maggs's 'ending' deserves further analysis. Many critics at the time of *Jack Maggs*'s publication declared themselves dissatisfied with the novel's 'happy ending'. But we need to register that Carey, like Fowles before him, is deeply self-aware about this impositional sense of narrative closure. In *The French Lieutenant's Woman* Fowles offered alternative endings, while acknowledging that 'the conventions of Victorian fiction allow, allowed, no place for the open, the inconclusive ending' (1996 [1969]: 38). *Great Expectations* is invariably published in modern editions with its own alternative endings, however; first, the quasi-happy ending imposed by Dickens's editor Bulwer Lytton, in which a strong hint is given that Pip and Estella might live happily ever after, and the darker ending Dickens initially preferred. There is then a Dickensian precedent for the false consciousness that surrounds Carey's 'happy ending' for Maggs, in which he and Mercy Larkin make a new life back in Australia (Porter 1997: 16; cited in ní Fhlathúin 1999: 91). As Woodcock observes there is a 'fairy tale, deliberately unreal' air to this section (2003: 137), with its idyllic depiction of happy families; none of what precedes this in the novel would seem to predict this outcome, and the atmosphere of unreality is compounded by the overall ending which refers to Mercy's collection of first editions of the novel about Maggs, *The Death of Maggs*. In an act of narrative circularity, the first time we see Mercy in this novel she is handling books in Percy Buckle's personal library. There is a fictional, a literary, aspect, then, to this ending which seems inescapable. Even the printed dedication to Buckle in *The Death of Maggs* appears false in view of what we have read previously. Texts can lie and mislead and Carey's fiction toys with this possibility throughout its narrative and retains its sceptical awareness of unstable textualities to its close.

Carey's appropriation of *Great Expectations* not only rewrites events in Dickens's canonical novel, it goes one step further by bringing a version of the author himself into the heart of the fiction. Tobias Oates, a journalist in the early stages of a career in novel writing, anxious for patronage and success, is a thinly concealed variation on what we know of Dickens's biography. Kate Flint has noted that Dickens wrote *Great Expectations* during a vexed moment in his personal life. On 11 March 1861, he wrote to a friend W. H. Wills that he felt 'quite weighed down and loaded and chained in life' (cited in Dickens 1994: x; Dickens 1938: 212). He had separated from his wife in 1858 and was the subject of considerable popular scandal surrounding his rumoured relationship with the actress Ellen Tiernan (Kaplan 1988: 416–17). The year 1861 was also an unsettled time on the world stage, witnessing as it did the outbreak of the American Civil War. Carey's fiction is interested in Dickens's troubled family life, but less with the relationship with 'Nelly' Tiernan, than in the hints earlier in Dickens's life of an affection verging on the obsessive for his wife's sister, Mary Hogarth. Mary died a tragic early death aged seventeen, and although Dickens was undeniably distraught at her death the vanity of his account of it is inescapable: 'Thank God she died in my arms ... and the very last words she whispered were of me' (Ackroyd 1990: 226).

In *Jack Maggs* Tobias Oates proves a vain, fairly reprehensible character, one who not only uses those around him as fodder for his fiction with little sense of ethical responsibility, but whose personal life renders his wife Mary (the slippage of Mary Hogarth's name into that of Oates's wife in *Jack Maggs* is surely deliberate on Carey's part) and her sister Lizzie Warrinder the victims of his egotism. Carey's fictional recreation of Dickens appears to owe much in this to the vain, if brilliant, individual depicted by Peter Ackroyd's monumental biography of the writer (1990). As well as these obvious parallels between Oates's life and what is known of Dickens's, *Jack Maggs* is structured around a series of parallels and echoes, both external and internal. There are several textual parallels with *Great Expectations*, internal echoes as it were, but also with other works in the Dickens *oeuvre*. The thieving community in which Maggs finds himself placed as a child is a version of Fagin's factory of child-thieves in *Oliver Twist*, for example. And Oates, we learn, uses the figure of Maggs in several of *his* future novels: 'Finally they slept, and Tobias Oates crept out. This scene, or rather the specifics of its setting, reappears not only in *The Death of Maggs* and *Michael Adams*, but in almost everything Tobias Oates ever wrote' (Carey 1997: 197).

Great Expectations is a narrative founded on the connections between things. Pip tries increasingly to keep the constituent parts of his life separate, embarrassed as he is when Joe Gargery visits him in London, feeling the world of the Kent marshes to be far behind him and irrelevant, compromising even, to his new existence as a gentleman. What Pip fails to realize is how intimately his new life is connected to his experiences in 'th' meshes' (Dickens 1994 [1861]: 222), enabled as it is by Magwitch's wealth and patronage. Other threads eventually connect in the novel when we learn that Maggs's arch-rival in crime, Compeyson, is the bridegroom who deserted Miss Havisham on her wedding day and that Estella is really Magwitch's child. The connectivity of Carey's novel is achieved both through the relationship between hypotext and hypertext and the parallels identified with Dickens's own life. There are also multiple parallels within the narrative. Oates in many respects becomes Maggs's shadow and counterpart, itself Carey's variation on the popular figure in nineteenth-century fiction of the *doppelganger* or double. Events in Maggs's and Oates's lives mirror each other with disturbing regularity. The harrowing abortion of Maggs's child with Sophia in Ma Britten's house, told in flashback within the narrative, itself a textual echo of Dickens's narrative structure in *Great Expectations* with its stories within stories, is mirrored by the fatal abortion induced by drugs administered to Lizzie, without each other's knowledge, by both Tobias and Mary. In turn, the manuscript of Oates's projected novel loosely based on Maggs's life which burns in the fire at

Maggs's behest prefigures the burning of Lizzie's bedsheets following her painful death (thereby also burning the aborted foetus, and effecting a disturbing connection between Oates's creative offspring).

Oates is also rendered a thief by the narrative as much as Maggs himself. Labels such as 'the convict' or 'the writer' become treacherously unstable in the course of *Jack Maggs* where, increasingly, they have the potential to apply to either Maggs or Oates: several of the inset narratives in the text, for example, are products of Maggs's impulse to write his life story for Henry Phipps. In a related slippage of textual certainty, Maggs eschews the label of 'Australian' that both Oates and in some respects Carey seem anxious to pin on him (Carey 1997: 312–13). Instead of the hallmarked silver that Maggs is trained as a child to steal, however, it is 'real' (Carey's narrative is equally hesitant about the labels of 'real' and 'fictional') lives that Oates plunders for the raw material of his fiction. Maggs describes his feeling of having been 'burgled' after the first episode of somnambulism, during which Oates makes careful notes of Maggs's outbursts about his life as an Australian convict to incorporate in his novel: 'He was burgled, plundered, and he would not tolerate it' (32). Oates, in a further direct parallel with Dickens's active fascination throughout his career with workings of the criminal mind, is a proponent of the nineteenth-century pseudo-science of mesmerism (Ackroyd 1990: 448–51). This has been viewed by some as a precursor of modern psychotherapy and in this way Carey parallels not only his modern method of psychologizing Dickens's convict, but also the acts of burglary and appropriation inherent to the imperialist ideology:

> The metafictional strategies of the novel are integral to the exposure of colonial delusions. They call attention to the process of fictional invention ... as appropriation, theft. Just as England stole Maggs's birthright by making him a thief, so Tobias Oates colonizes Maggs for his own imaginative purposes, stealing Maggs's life for his fiction.
>
> (Woodcock 2003: 129)

There is an overriding anxiety for the reader of *Jack Maggs* as there is for the reader of *Wide Sargasso Sea* that the protagonists may prove unable to escape the plot trajectories determined for them by their names and literary counterparts. The sense Pip has in *Great Expectations* that

Magwitch cannot escape his initial identification as a convict has obvious implications for the former's attempts to escape his life with Joe at the forge:

> The more I dressed him and the better I dressed him, the more he looked like the slouching fugitive on the marshes. This effect on my anxious fancy was partly referable, no doubt, to his old face and manner growing more familiar to me; but I believed too that he dragged one of his legs as if there were still a weight of iron on it, and that from head to foot there was Convict in the very grain of the man.
>
> (Dickens 1994 [1861]: 333)

Carey enjoys considering his character's ability to rewrite his destiny. In one central encounter in a moving carriage, and one that self-consciously echoes Fowles's encounter with his protagonist in a train compartment in *The French Lieutenant's Woman*, Carey has Maggs confront Oates over the novel he is writing and challenge the vindictive end he has in mind for the character based on his life. As we have already seen, Carey also rewrites Maggs's end; his Australian deathbed scene in old age acting as a counterpart for that envisaged for him by Oates. The title of Oates's novel is determined by this fate, *The Death of Maggs*; the death by fire is, of course, a reworking in turn of Miss Havisham's demise in the Dickensian source. The fantasy element of that ending, however, leaves us in some considerable doubt as to how free Maggs can get from his textual shackles.

What Carey does achieve for his character is to make him centre stage in the way he could never be in *Great Expectations* since that narrative was voiced through the first person observation and perspective of Pip. Carey's novel about Maggs/Magwitch is deliberately eponymous. The image Carey deploys on regular occasion in the narrative to signify this centralizing move is the bringing of Maggs out of the shadows. As in much nineteenth-century fiction, and many of the appropriations we have been looking at in this chapter, not least Fowles's *The French Lieutenant's Woman* and Wilson's *The Dark Clue*, London is a vibrant but double-sided entity in this novel, a metropolis of gas-lights and side-streets, a place of fine houses but also alley-ways and back passages, the lit and the unlit. It is the latter spaces that Maggs is frequently seen skulking in or emerging from. Carey quite literally brings his character's experiences out of the shadows and into the light. And elsewhere this is a novel concerned with subtexts and subterranean truths; Henry Phipps, Pip's dark counterpart or *doppelganger* in *Jack Maggs*, is guilty of violently sodomizing the footman Edward Constable and causing the suicide of Constable's partner. In other ways Oates violates Maggs's life and thoughts in a gothic representation of the novelist's art. Carey is in this way making explicit what can often only exist as the subtextual or implied in Victorian fiction, be it colonialism, sexual repression, or violence. In this way, Carey's narrative brilliantly 'vents' the world of the Victorian novel and the Dickensian idiom but the light he brings to bear on his subject is inescapably modern.

8

STRETCHING HISTORY; OR, APPROPRIATING THE FACTS

The author willingly admits to having once or twice stretched history to
suit his own fictional ends.

Peter Carey's 'Author's Note' to *Jack Maggs*

Up 'until this point we have been discussing adaptation and appropriation within the intertextual framework of texts adopting and adapting
other texts. In the next and final chapter, following Kristeva's lead in
her writing on intertextuality in *Desire in Language* (1980), we expand
the parameters of that debate to include the companion art forms of
painting and music. But there is a further parallel mode of appropriation that uses as its raw material not literary or artistic matter but the
'real' matter of facts, of historical events and personalities. What happens, then, to the appropriation process when what is being 'taken over'
for fictional purpose really exists or existed?

The kinds of literature we are examining under this heading are
often grouped together by means of the generic title of 'historical fiction'. But historical fiction is a wide umbrella term. It can, for example,
include novels or plays which choose to locate themselves in the 'past',
known or otherwise, providing contextual details of that 'past' as an
authenticating strategy: we 'believe in' or yield to the events of such
novels or plays partly because the background detail is so accurately
drawn. There are separate studies to be made of the larger impulse

towards the writing of historical fiction, but of more obvious and pressing concern to this study are those texts where the author is consciously appropriating the known facts of a particular event or of a particular life in order to shape their fiction. Their motives in doing so can vary. In some instances, a historical event is depicted and deployed both for its own rich literary and imaginative content and for the parallels and comparisons it evokes with more contemporary or topical concerns. One of the best-known examples of this from the theatrical canon is Arthur Miller's 1953 play, *The Crucible*. That play represents the events surrounding the witch-hunts conducted in 1692 among the New England Puritan colony of Salem. It is an empathetic study of the personal rivalries and psychological disorders that contributed to the rampant accusations of witchcraft against the women, and eventually men, of that community, and which led to several gruesome public executions. But Miller's purpose in selecting this particular moment in history for his drama was twofold. While he was clearly interested in the group hysteria and religious ardour that contributed to the Salem executions, he also sought to promote in his audiences' imaginations a direct comparison with the contemporary 'witch-hunts' being conducted in his native USA in the 1950s by Senator Joe McCarthy and his supporters. Via the mechanism of the House of Representatives' House Un-American Activities Committee (HUAC), this group was hell-bent on exposing communism within US society. Those in the performing arts, actors, directors, and playwrights among them, were a particular focus of surveillance and public show-trials in which they were encouraged to inform on their colleagues. Miller was himself sentenced to prison in 1957 for his failure to act as an informant for HUAC, although the sentence was later quashed (Bigsby 1997: 3). Nowhere in the play script does *The Crucible* make this modern analogue explicit; Miller simply trusts his audience to draw their own conclusions. Of course, audiences today come to the play with prior knowledge of the historical and political analogue, but *The Crucible* remains an impressive example of a historical past being evoked in a literary context as a means of critiquing, albeit obliquely, the present political regime. What Miller was doing was, of course, nothing new: William Shakespeare and Ben Jonson achieved something remarkably similar in England in the early seventeenth century when they deployed the setting and stories of Ancient

Rome as a means of escaping the censor and yet critiquing present governmental policies.

Ronan Bennett has also recently evoked seventeenth-century society and its atmosphere of religious fervour and fundamentalism in his novel *Havoc in its Third Year* (2003). Set in Northern England in the 1630s, the decade preceding the outbreak of the civil wars, Bennett depicts a town where the restrictive Puritan leadership has created a world of paranoia and surveillance where neighbour is turned against neighbour, often with fatal consequences. The parallels between the world depicted in the novel and the rise of religious fundamentalism that took place in both Muslim and Christian communities in the early twenty-first century, not least in the wake of the events and political aftermaths of 9/11, proved inescapable for readers and reviewers alike.

History can often be evoked, then, for the purposes of comparison or contrast. But as Peter Widdowson has stressed 'there are many ways in which "the literary" uses history, and many ends to which it is put' (1999: 154). At various points in this book, we have had cause to evoke postmodernism's questioning of the past, and of so-called historical 'facts'. Jean Rhys appropriates Charlotte Brontë's *Jane Eyre* in *Wide Sargasso Sea* in order to reveal the embedded racism of the British imperial age and its literature; Peter Carey rewrites Dickens's *Great Expectations* in *Jack Maggs* in order to highlight gaps and absences in Dickens's, and by extension the Victorian era's, concerns: the life of those transported to the penal colony of Australia. History, literary or otherwise, is being redeployed in these instances in order to indicate those communities and individuals whose histories have not been told before, the marginalized and the disenfranchised as represented by Rhys's Antoinette or Carey's Maggs. Don DeLillo achieves the related effect in *Libra* (1988) of seeing an iconic historical event, the assassination of President John F. Kennedy in Dallas in 1963, not just from the perspective of the identified assassin Lee Harvey Oswald, but via the interior voices and mindset of others in his life. What is revealed in the process is a world of poverty and disenfranchisement that is often missing from the conspiracy-led historical accounts of that shooting.

The retrieval of lost or repressed voices is a motif we have identified as being common to many of the appropriations we have considered thus far. In prose fiction re-visions of Shakespearean plays, such as *The*

Tempest in Marina Warner's *Indigo* or *King Lear* in Jane Smiley's *A Thousand Acres*, which both deploy first person narration, a conscious effort is made to give a voice, and in turn a set of comprehensible motives, to characters either marginalized on, or completely absent from, the Shakespearean stage. A shared purpose can in this respect be identified in much postmodern historical fiction, or historiographic metafiction as it is sometimes called, that deploys the technique of first person narration. Peter Carey's *True History of the Kelly Gang* (2000), for example, has been praised as a remarkable achievement of ventriloquism. Certainly Carey vividly supplies the idiom, slang, and idiosyncratic punctuation that suggest we are receiving Ned Kelly's 'voice' direct. The novel is structured as a series of letters written by Kelly to his daughter in order to ensure that she hears the story from him as well as others. For this reason 'parcels' of letters substitute for chapters in this self-aware novel. Carey confidently plays with the methods of recording archival detail in the framing authorial introduction to each 'parcel': '59 octavo pages all of high wood-pulp content and turning brown. Folds, foxing, staining and minor tears' (2000: 73). This framing material achieves two conflicting ends within the narrative. It serves as an authenticating presence; as readers we are trained to trust the historical evidence of archival material catalogued in this way. Yet these frames also serve as a reminder of historical voices and interpreters other than Kelly himself; we are, by this method, reminded that postmodernism's favoured strategy of unreliable narration may be relevant in Ned's case. As much as he is mythologized in Australian history books as that nation's version of the Robin Hood legend, a poor man of Irish provenance who suffered intense racism and who took on the authorities in several daring raids and sieges, Kelly may also be rewriting his own history, censoring certain 'truths' or embellishing others in view of his intended audience of his daughter.

The title of Carey's novel performs a similar sleight of hand: *True History of the Kelly Gang* would seem at first sight to emphasize the veracity of this version of the story, told as it is from the gang's point of view. Yet Carey has self-consciously avoided the use of a definite article here – it is not *the* true history. This identifiable absence suggests that we need to question the phrase 'true history'. An alert reader may even suspect an oxymoronic quality to the term, since, as much late twentieth-century scholarship was at pains to point out, history itself is often simply one person's assessment and interpretation of events from the available or extant documents and evidential traces left behind. What happens to those, such as Ned Kelly's immediate family for example, whose illiteracy reduced their capacity to leave behind textual traces of their existence; how does history speak for or about them? Carey, as in his earlier *Jack Maggs*, is concerned in this novel with offering a voice to these lost voices; as Bruce Woodcock notes, Carey's fictions 'are inhabited by hybrid characters living in in-between spaces or on the margins' (2003: 1), adding that 'They retell the stories of marginalized characters, outsiders, and outlaws ... in reinvented voices' (138). Woodcock has memorably described this less as ventriloquism than 'a performative act of habitation, occupation' (2003: 138). By appropriating Kelly's life-story, Carey enacts appropriation's semantic meaning by carrying out an 'occupation' or 'takeover' but this is not a hostile act; he is anxious to give a voice to the lives of the poor whom he sees as having been marginalized in and by the historical record. His model for this is undoubtedly the American author William Faulkner, who also provides the epigram to this novel: 'The past is not dead. It is not even past.'

It is important to grasp that Carey is 'reinventing' history, as well as retrieving voices he deems to have been suppressed by history as a formal discipline. The phrase 'true history' not only connects his project to the practice of historical research and interpretation but also to the art of fiction. In the seventeenth century, many prose novellas and romances declared themselves to be 'true histories' in this manner, while simultaneously connecting themselves as much to the conventions of romantic writing as to actual historical event or personages (cf. Woodcock 2003: 142): Aphra Behn's *Oroonoko, or The Royal Slave* (1688) and *The Unfortunate Happy Lady: A True History* (1698) are facilitating examples. Behn plays on the etymological connection between the word 'history' and the French term for a 'story' or fiction, *histoire*, in a manner that prefigures and pre-empts much of postmodernism's playful encounters with the discipline.

By devising a novel constructed from letters Carey simultaneously evokes the modes of truth and fiction. His inspiration for the novel came from witnessing a genuine Kelly-authored document of this kind, which in turn evokes the parallel genre of biography; and yet further informing models are clearly those of the eighteenth-century fictional forms of epistolary and picaresque novels. History is not being undone by means of these appropriations and adaptations, but its stability is being questioned. As Linda Hutcheon observes: 'Postmodernism does not deny [history] ... it merely questions how we can know past real events, today, except through their traces, their texts, the facts we construct and to which we grant meaning ...' (1988: 225). Carey seems acutely aware of these 'traces' and the complex and questioning ways in which we must handle them in the construction of his novel.

It is through the framing device of the third person narration of events following Kelly's execution, and the voicing of the reaction of the man entrusted with Kelly's manuscripts, that Carey seems to hint at one of his own motives when appropriating history for this novel. Curnow asks enviously: 'What is it about we Australians, eh? ... What is wrong with us? Do we not have a Jefferson? A Disraeli? Might we not find someone better to admire than a horse-thief and a murderer? Must we always make such an embarrassing spectacle of ourselves?' (2000: 419). Kelly's iconic fame in Australia, in large part deriving from the mode and manner of his death, seems to confirm Jean Baudrillard's claim that history has transmuted into myth in the modern era and that early death accrues a particularly mythic dimension. Baudrillard cites the specific examples of Marilyn Monroe, James Dean, and JFK (1981: 24), declaring: 'History is our lost referential, that is to say our myth' (43). Carey is certainly questioning the mythologizing process and yet he is not on Curnow's side in the novel either. In the same way that his postcolonial re-vision of *Great Expectations* found empathy for the convict community of New South Wales so here he seeks motive and reason, and the understanding of the reader, for Kelly's life and actions.

Just as the appropriation of a canonical novel relies upon the reader's foreknowledge of the precursor text for a full appreciation of its questions and potential for critique, its revisionary achievement as it were, so the appropriation of Kelly's life in *True History of the Kelly Gang* relies upon a reader's awareness, albeit in outline, of his life and the mythology surrounding it. Carey uses this to create a sense of predestination in the novel akin to the awareness of the plot trajectory of a canonical drama or novel; in a sense, both we as readers and Kelly writing his personal history know how it will end. Carey ensures this even for the uninitiated by opening the novel with the shoot-out that led to Kelly's arrest and eventual execution. The iconic signifier of his hand-crafted armour, and his assumed persona of the 'Monitor' (the name derives from the goanna, or monitor lizard, an inhabitant of Australia's rain-forests), immediately locate the reader in terms of the historical record. Like Jean Rhys's Antoinette, Ned's life is shaped by our awareness of his end; as Woodcock observes: 'Ned is dogged by a sense of fatalism and destiny. Unlike Jack Maggs, Carey's Ned Kelly seems trapped by the script history has written for him and, despite his hope that he will be able to read his account in the future with his daughter in America, he is all too aware of his coming doom ...' (2003: 150).

Another novel that both appropriates a historical life and a mythology, and begins with the tragic end of its protagonist, is Joyce Carol Oates's *Blonde*, her 'fantasy biography' (the phrase is Hilary Mantel's, quoted in the paperback edition of the novel) of cinema icon Norma Jeane Baker, better known by her film name of Marilyn Monroe. Monroe's life (and death), as mentioned above, are singled out for mythical status by Baudrillard's *Simulacra and Simulation* (1981), and Oates is clearly relying on her readership's shared perception of Monroe's iconographic status in the construction of her novel. In her authorial preface, Oates asserts that '*Blonde* is a radically distilled "life" in the form of fiction, and ... synecdoche is the principle of appropriation' (2000: ix). The cover of the first paperback edition of the novel in the UK seemed to emphasize Oates's point: it depicted a fragment of an iconic photograph of Monroe, one actually described in the novel, a still taken as a publicity shot for the film *Bus Stop*. The chapter in question is entitled: '"The American Goddess of Love on the Subway Grating", New York City 1954':

> A lush-bodied girl in the prime of her physical beauty. In an ivory geor-gette crepe sundress with a halter top that gathers her breasts up in soft undulating folds of the fabric. She's standing with bare legs apart on a New York subway grating. Her blond hair is thrown rapturously back as an updraft lifts her full flaring skirt.
>
> (Oates 2000: 601)

The fragment we are given as consumers of the novel, however, is just a glimpse of Monroe's platinum blonde hair from that photographic image. The 'blonde' of the title is enough to connote Marilyn, with the added irony, of course, that her blonde was itself an act of fakery and self-fashioning in the context of Hollywood's creation of her image. Oates captures a crucial point about appropriation here: synecdoche *is* the principle of the form in respect that it relies on simple signifiers to tell larger stories: a wisp of peroxide blonde is enough to suggest the myth and iconicity of Marilyn Monroe and the attendant tragedies of her personal life, in the same way that for Peter Carey Ned Kelly's home-made 'Monitor' armour conjures up a comparable mythology. In Jean Rhys's *Wide Sargasso Sea* an English stately home and a candle is enough to suggest the fire at Thornfield Hall in *Jane Eyre*. In *Blonde* Oates's self-conscious nomenclature relies on the reader's knowledge of the 'facts' of Monroe's biography; we are introduced to several unnamed but nevertheless recognizable players in her life: the 'Ex-Athlete' is Joe Di Maggio; the sexually tyrannical 'President' is John F. Kennedy (although there were also important topical parallels with the Bill Clinton–Monica Lewinsky affair when Oates's novel was published); 'O' is Laurence Olivier; the 'Playwright' is Arthur Miller. The postmodern reader is alert to these signifiers, to the semantic interplay between the source they conjure up and the rewriting that surrounds these fragmentary evocations of a real-life precursor of the events described.

Like Carey's *True History of the Kelly Gang*, Oates's *Blonde* starts at the end, with Monroe's death, around which conspiracy theories have swirled. Once again a reader's foreknowledge and expectation is a crucial element in the construction of the narrative dynamic. We are participants in the act of appropriation, persistently reading between the lines. A parallel effect is achieved by another Joyce Carol Oates novel that appropriates an actual historical event, *Black Water* (1993). That text's factual hypotext is the so-called Chappaquiddick tragedy, another story-line involving a member of the Kennedy dynasty, Senator Edward Kennedy. In the actual event, which occurred in 1969, Mary-Jo Kopechne drowned in a car driven by Kennedy. He was later found guilty of having left the scene of an accident, though many questions remain as to exactly how Kopechne died. What remains clear is that Kennedy's hopes of securing his party's presidential nomination, which had seemed high until this incident, also drowned in the marsh water of Cape Cod that July night. In Oates's novel events are transposed to

Maine in the 1990s. This historical setting is carefully signified by discussion of Michel Dukakis's failed presidential campaign against George Bush Sr in 1988. Nevertheless the narrative's account of the power- and sex-hungry 'Senator', the drowning of Kelly Kelleher, and the resultant cover-up to protect his presidential hopes unmistakeably calls to mind the events in Chappaquiddick. As with Miller's *The Crucible*, Oates relies on the alert reader's recognition of the story's 'real-life' counterparts. The jacket of the paperback edition of the book emphasizes this intention with its reference to 'a shocking story that has become an American myth', without ever specifically naming Chappaquiddick.

The narrative of *Black Water* is brilliantly structured in the form of an interior monologue, taking place inside Kelly's head during the minutes, or hours, in which she drowns. The novel is deliberately ambivalent about time; we know that Kelly has found an air-pocket in the submerged vehicle, but there remains the possibility that she is seeing her life flash before her eyes in the seconds before she dies. The sections which occur in a rush of words with minimal or no punctuation underlines this terrifying possibility. The verbal refrains also serve to emphasize that, for all the rewriting of Oates's project, the end is inescapable: 'Just before the car flew off the road'; 'As the black water filled her lungs and she died'.

Oates's project can be compared to Carey's *True History of the Kelly Gang* in the sense that she appropriates the story of the Chappaquiddick incident, forging history into fiction, in an effort to give back a voice to the silenced Mary-Jo Kopechne. There is a conscious effort to retrieve a lost history here too, to see Kopechne's life with its own value and not just as an appendix to the Kennedy family myth. In the narrative, Kelly even reflects on the fact that you never doubt you will be able to tell your own story. In this way Oates allows the novel to speak for her in a way the historical record cannot. The discipline of history, as we have seen on countless occasions in this study, is in truth a history of textualities, of stories told by particular tellers according to particular ideologies and contexts (see, for example, White 1987). In this sense, history proves a ripe source and intertext for fiction, for *histoire*, to appropriate.

9

APPROPRIATING THE ARTS AND SCIENCES

Literature has found endless inspiration in canonical works of art as well as literature. Tracy Chevalier's *Girl with a Pearl Earring* (1999) creates a history for the enigmatic woman represented in Johannes Vermeer's remarkable painting of the same name, and that same author has recently carried out a similar exercise in fiction with the famous medieval tapestries of the Musée National du Moyen Age (Cluny Museum) in her *The Lady and the Unicorn* (2003). Julian Barnes uses as his inspirational springboard in *A History of the World in 10½ Chapters* (1989) Géricault's 'The Raft of Medusa' (as well as the biblical parable of Noah's ark). In *The Dark Clue* (2001, the novel is discussed in Chapter 7), James Wilson embeds several allusions to Turner's paintings within the action of the novel. This is an extension of the impulse to read between the lines or fill in the gaps that we have seen in practice in much of the literature that appropriates canonical writing. In each instance the author relies on the reader's foreknowledge of the work of art that is being alluded to and appropriated for the purposes of the narrative.

Michael Frayn's *Headlong* (1999) achieves something similar, if even more embedded, with its deployment of Pieter Breughel's remarkable painting of the 'Fall of Icarus', in which Icarus's demise is famously off-centre, marginalized to the corner of the frame. Combining a researcher's knowledge of Breughel with the conventions of a mystery novel or detective fiction, Frayn has his art-dealer protagonist (wrongly) believe he has discovered a lost painting that will make his fortune. En route, Frayn has great fun paralleling the pride of his overweening narrator with the fate of Icarus. This is, of course, far from the first time that Breughel's painting has been the subject of literary attention: W. H. Auden's poem 'Musée des Beaux Arts' captures beautifully the painting's decentring of the myth of overreaching ambition in its account of the work's depiction of the everyday events onland carrying on heedless of Icarus's demise out at sea.

Appropriation clearly extends far beyond the adaptation of other texts into new literary creations, assimilating both historical lives and events, as viewed in the preceding chapter, and companion art forms, as mentioned above, into the process. Painting, portraiture, photography, film, and musical composition all become part of the rich treasury of 'texts' available to the adaptor. This is nothing new as such; it is a process that has been underway for centuries and which has manifested itself across many cultures. Nevertheless, it has gained a particular cadence and significance in the wake of the late twentieth-century postmodernist theory, which has made us constantly aware of the processes of intervention and interpretation involved in any relationship or engagement with existent art forms.

Postmodernism has troubled over the replacement of the 'real' by exact reproductions or imitations. In our evermore skilful capacity to reproduce or clone objects and art forms in the age of mass production and reproduction, these imitations take on a 'hyper-real' quality. Jean Baudrillard offers one of the more expansive ruminations on this theme in his account of simulation and simulacra in the modern era (1981), but perhaps the seminal account remains Walter Benjamin's hugely influential essay 'The Work of Art in the Age of Technological Reproducibility' (Benjamin 2003b [1935]: 4.252). This essay, previously better known by the title 'The Work of Art in the Age of Mechanical Reproduction', suggested a loss of 'aura' in the modern age of reproduction and cloning. Benjamin did not necessarily regard this as a negative outcome. Indeed, in a formulation relevant for our accounts of the adaptive process, he suggested that the attendant deconstruction of 'aura' freed texts in their afterlives from the stranglehold of the original (Eagleton 1994 [1981]: 40; Ferris 2004: 47). His productive resolution of the dichotomous relationship between originality and repetition which has troubled T. S. Eliot, Harold Bloom, and legal theorists alike (see Gaines 1991: 64) is important for the discussions that both precede and follow in this volume.

Returning, in the light of Benjamin's theory, to Eliot's notion of tradition and the individual talent, we need, perhaps, to effect a paramount shift away from the idea of authorial originality towards a more collaborative and societal understanding of the production of art and the production of meaning. Richard Powers suggests as much in his response to new technology in the wake of Benjamin's theories in his novel *Three Farmers on Their Way to a Dance*. Dissecting photography and film's ability to enable a collective, democratized form of history, by according the masses the power to select and record the moment, he observes:

> a new technology, already on us, extends this ability well beyond still photography. Every home is about to be transformed into an editing studio, with books, prints, films, and tapes serving the new-age viewer as little more than rough cuts to be assembled and expanded into customized narratives. Reproduction will make the creation and appreciation of works truly interactive.
>
> (Powers 2001 [1985]: 260)

It is certainly the interactive quality of appropriative art that emerges with most force from the studies conducted here; this serves in turn to question any bland account of meaning being evacuated from postmodernist art and literature purely by dint of its imitative or recursive qualities.

Andy Warhol's artistic output has often served as a crucial touchstone in debates about the evacuation of meaning in postmodern derivative art. His 'multiples', repeated, screen-printed images of twentieth-century icons ranging from Elvis Presley to Mao Tse-Tung to Marilyn Monroe, are an interesting case study. What the reproductive, adaptive element in Warhol's artworks achieves is to underscore the iconicity, and therefore duplicability, of such images ('brands') in the age of mechanical reproduction, but that does not mean that his work is simply evacuated of meaning in the process. His 'multiples' comment on the power and glamour of celebrity and fame in the modern era; by extension, they subject Monroe's image to the kind of synecdochal appropriation explored in detail by Joyce Carol Oates in her novel *Blonde*, discussed in the previous chapter.

Monroe's image is an interesting case since it raises the concomitant issues of copyright and ownership that have provided a backdrop to many of the discussions of adaptation in this volume. Legal theorist Rosemary Coombes has examined attempts made by the pop singer Madonna to copyright her image in the lawcourts. The difficulty comes with the allusive and referential quality of Madonna's own image, which has invoked Monroe's film career and physical appearance on numerous occasions: in the video for her recording of 'Material Girl' for example Madonna consciously imitates Monroe's performance of the song 'Diamonds are a Girl's Best Friend' in *Gentlemen Prefer Blondes* (1951). If Madonna trademarks her appearance, which is recognizably derivative of Monroe's, what are the legal implications? Coombes contests:

> If the Madonna image appropriates the likenesses of earlier screen god-desses, religious symbolism, feminist rhetoric, and sadomasochistic fantasy to speak to contemporary sexual aspirations and anxieties then the value of the image derives as much, perhaps, from the collective cultural heritage on which she draws as from her individual efforts. But if we grant Madonna exclusive property rights in her image, we simultaneously make it difficult for others to appropriate those same resources for new ends, and we freeze the Madonna constellation itself.
>
> (1994: 107–8)

From the standpoint of contract law, Coombes argues for greater flexibility in our approach to the artistic form, proposing a strategy whereby we would move away from the assignment of specific individual copyrights towards acceptance of the fact that a fundamental part of the artistic process is adaptation and (re)interpretation. Without this flexibility, artistic access to the public domain will become choked by the need for consent. Jane Gaines makes a parallel argument about 'iconic similarity' in her book *Contested Images* (1991: xvi).

The artist Cindy Sherman has deliberately provoked similar debates about originality and authenticity in her photographic reworkings of iconic Renaissance paintings (Cruz *et al.* 1997). There is both fidelity and infidelity simultaneously at work in her photograph of herself in the position of a Caravaggio subject (see, for example, her reworking of

'Boy bitten by a lizard'). She has shifted genre, from fine art to photography, so on no level can this be straightforward copying; and she raises issues of gender and representation by means of the substitution of herself for Caravaggio's boy model. The work is 'hers', then, in so far as it raises questions and applications that depend entirely on her intervention into the original artwork to which the photograph refers, and upon which further meanings will be layered by the gaze of the observer of the photograph in new cultural conditions and contexts. There is in some sense a historical return taking place here, a return to the freedom of imitation, borrowing, assimilation, and *bricolage* witnessed in the works of Shakespeare and his contemporaries in the early modern period, and a move away from the legal definitions of plagiarism and copyright infringement which dominate the modern era. It is a controversial and contested opinion but one which raises central ideas about creative freedom that we would do well to ponder.

Discussing the function of the author, Michel Foucault suggested that the value placed on 'authorship' in the creative process tended to end up by denying intertextuality (1979: 20). What is sought in any artistic argument against 'individual rights' in or ownership of a particular image or pose is a more collaborative, societal understanding or definition of both production and reproduction: 'The very concept of authorship overrides the generic and conventional indebtedness that would mark works as the product not so much of individuals as societies' (Gaines 1991: 77). It is this collaborative production of cultural meaning, not least in the practice of history, that Richard Powers interrogates in *Three Farmers on Their Way to a Dance*. That novel commences with not one but two suggestive artworks: Diego Rivera's Henry Ford-commissioned murals in Detroit, both an homage to and a terrifying portrayal of, as Powers reads it, the age of the machine, and August Sander's evocative and yet enigmatic photograph of three young farmers on their way to a village dance, taken in 1914 when Europe stood poised on the brink of change in the face of the terrible collective trauma of the Great War. Powers's novel and narrator are anxious to imagine a history for these three unnamed men who would have been conscripted into the Prussian army within months of the photograph being taken. In a creative move akin to those authors we have looked at who have sought to retrieve the lost voices of literature and history, Powers is writing a story into the historical gaps and *lacunae* offered up by the few known facts about this photograph. By further interweaving in his narrative the narrator's reflection on the perceiver's, and by extension the historian's and the biographer's, interventionist role in reading meaning into this image with a third plotline of an American IT worker who finds a personal connection to this photograph, Powers makes a powerful case for the collaborative production of artistic effect and historical knowledge, for, as he terms it, 'the impossibility of knowing where knowledge leaves off and involvement begins' (2001 [1985]: 206). Reflecting that 'describing and altering are two inseparable parts of the same process ...' (206), Powers asserts that 'there can be no interpretation without participating ...' (207). It is this crucial notion of participation, cultural, social, and ethical, that I wish to suggest, and hope to have indicated in the examples cited in this volume, adaptation and appropriation represent and perform as artistic and aesthetic processes.

It would be dangerous, of course, to imply that the line of influence is entirely one-directional: painting and photography have enjoyed an allusive intertextual relationship with literature as well. The paintings of the Pre-Raphaelites in the nineteenth century endlessly reworked scenes and images from Shakespearean drama, often realizing visually events that only occur off-stage in the plays themselves, such as Ophelia's florally bedecked drowning as described by Gertrude in 4.7.138–55 of *Hamlet*, and depicted so memorably by John Everett Millais. Angela Carter's revisitation of Ophelia's death in several of her novels and short stories, it has been argued, is as much influenced by Millais's evocative painting as by the Shakespearean verse description (Sage 1994: 33). Jonathan Bate has also registered Laurence Olivier's self-conscious 'remake' of this image in a cinematic generic context when he filmed the play in 1948 (Bate 1997: 266). Pre-Raphaelite art in turn influenced the theatricalized photographic tableaux of Julia Margaret Cameron, whose work also influenced the forays into fiction of Virginia Woolf, in particular her 1941 novel *Between the Acts* which sees a group of actors producing historical *tableaux* on a provincial village stage. As connections and interconnections of these kinds proliferate in our argument, we need, perhaps, to think less in terms of lines of influence and more in terms of webs or networks of allusion and (mutual) influence.

Music has also found an important reference point in canonical literature. Opera, ballet, and musical, as mentioned in Chapter 1, have looked to the Shakespearean canon and to fairy tale and mythology, among many other sources, for the plotlines and raw material for their own creative outputs. Musicology has had a long-standing interest in the practice of adaptation and appropriation, and much of the terminology that we have deployed when discussing literary adaptation resurfaces in this context: version, interpretation, replication, imitation, variation. But there are some subtle differences in the semantics that deserve mention. In the musical context words that might in a strictly literary sphere be taken to suggest direct copying without alteration undergo a shift of register, implying instead the kind of simultaneous acts of interpretation that Richard Powers suggests are the true mode of the reader's or spectator's response to art. In musicology, for example, replication refers not to a simple cloning of a precursor tune or tonal pattern, but a repetition played at one or more octaves above or below the precursor tone; a musical 'version' is a recognized 'variant' on a previously existent form, musical or otherwise; and 'imitation' means not unproblematic mimesis, a copy or counterfeit without alteration, addition or interpolation, as it is sometimes taken to mean in the literary context, but the repetition of a musical phrase in a different pitch. I have argued elsewhere in this volume for the possibilities opened up by deploying the terms of musicology when discussing the processes of adaptation and appropriation, and once again these kinetic definitions of phrases which in literary study have tended to become stultified or overly static in their application are hugely helpful.

Music has fed into the pages of fiction in an equally rich and informative way. E. M. Forster's evocation of Beethoven's Fifth Symphony at the heart of his novel *Howard's End* is a case in point. The music is literally experienced in the narrative in the form of the concert jointly attended by the Schlegel sisters and impoverished clerk Leonard Bast, but it also serves as a central metaphor and shaping movement in Forster's text. Helen Schlegel warns us early on both as readers and interpreters of the symphony to 'look out for the part where you think you have done with the goblins and they come back' (1985 [1910]: 46) and Forster makes determined space for the 'goblin footfalls' of the musical composition within his own narrative.

Richard Powers's *The Gold Bug Variations* makes comparable use of Bach's *Goldberg Variations*, a musical sequence evoked elsewhere in this volume as an example of the process of adaptation made into art form. Powers's novel does not appropriate Bach alone; his title puns on the popular name for Bach's composition and on Edgar Allan Poe's short story 'The Gold-Bug'. That story has at its heart a cracked cipher or decoded mystery. This connects with Powers's scientific concerns in his novel, which looks at the race to crack the genetic code of DNA in the earlier part of the twentieth century. His novel takes variation, then, as its central theme. On the surface an interweaving of two love stories, the narrative structure deliberately imitates the intertwined patterns of the double helix structure of DNA. Powers's writing persistently inter-weaves and connects scientific and artistic models. The actual cracking of the cipher of DNA by Francis Crick and James Watson, and its pub-lication in essay form, is described with great poetic beauty in *The Gold Bug Variations*: 'The piece breaks his heart with poignancy. It is a beauti-ful late twentieth-century pilgrim's narrative – exegesis pressing out-wards ...' (Powers 1991: 481).

The theory of DNA is all about correspondences and consonances, but perhaps even more importantly Powers finds correspondences between the patterns of variation in Bach's Goldberg compositions and the pat-terns of genetic adaptation that are in many respects the story told by the double helix. In Chapter 7 we argued for the Darwinian model of envi-ronmental adaptation as an important analogue to the literary practice of adaptation and in the double helix Powers finds a twentieth-century sci-entific equivalent. In the process, he argues for an enlarged understand-ing of a term like 'translation', and by extension our understanding of adaptation and reworking: 'The aim is not to extend the source but to widen the target, to embrace more than was possible before ... variation grows rich in a new tongue' (1991: 491). In Powers's account, art, like science, for all its intertextuality, proves to be less about echoes, repeti-tions, or rephrasings, however fundamental these are in practice, than about the identification of shared codes and possibilities. The discovery of these codes enables acts of endless (re)creativity in new contexts.

Part of the journey or pilgrimage of this book has been to find a means of discussing and interpreting adaptation and appropriation as literary and artistic processes that transcend the rather static or immobilizing discussion of source or influence that has sometimes hampered the study of texts produced in this domain. Current audiences for film and popular music are highly adept at invoking the processes and effects of intertextuality. Quotation, allusion, parody, and pastiche are all dominant modes in popular cultural programmes such as *The Simpsons* and *South Park*. With readerships and audiences already well honed in the art of searching for wider referential frameworks and contexts for the material they are receiving we need in turn to develop a more dynamic theoretical vocabulary to describe and mobilize these processes of response.

In searching for more kinetic models and terminology to provide the 'new critical idiom' for studying these forms, musicology has proved a particularly helpful discipline, offering us templates and paradigms as diverse and suggestive as baroque variation on grounds and the riffs and improvisational qualities of jazz. Science, too, in particular the theories of adaptation expounded by Mendel, by Darwin, and by those who have deployed the theories of Crick and Watson, has provided an equally potent reference point. It seems fitting therefore to move towards our conclusion with these recurring, yet innovative, patterns of Bach and DNA uppermost in our minds.

AFTERWORD

This exploration of literary adaptation and appropriation has had recourse at several points to companion art forms, such as film and music, and to the scientific domain, especially to those theories of genetic inheritance and environmental adaptation that began with Gregor Mendel and Charles Darwin in the nineteenth century and whose tendrils reach well into the twenty-first with the ongoing debates about DNA and genetic modification (Tudge 2002). Contemporary science talks about the modern synthesis of Mendel's theories of inheritance and Darwin's notions of diversity and variation in neo-Darwinism and this synthesis of ideas has had very genuine outcomes in the field of molecular biology and research into DNA. While acknowledging that a volume on the literary processes of adaptation and appropriation can only ever deploy such complex thinking at the level of metaphor and suggestion, nevertheless the Mendel–Darwin synthesis offers a useful way of thinking about the happy combination of influence and creativity, of tradition and the individual talent, and of parental influence and offspring, in appropriative literature, perhaps in all literature. In his autobiography, Darwin reflected on the 'endless beautiful adaptations that we everyday meet with' (cited in Beer 1983: 39). It can only be hoped that the aesthetic picture painted here has been one of comparable beauty, richness, and potential.

This is a 'Conclusion' or an 'Afterword', as I have preferred to term it, albeit one which is deeply conscious that its discussion cannot aim towards closure or summing up, but only gesture outwards towards future possibilities and ongoing adaptational processes. By opting for the phrase 'Afterword' I am conscious of how many appropriations have positioned themselves in relation to precursors via this notion of coming 'after', behind, in the shadows, or in the wake, of something else. John Gross has recently edited an anthology of Shakespearean appropriations entitled *After Shakespeare* (2000); Patrick Marber's English relocation and updating of Strindberg's influential 1888 naturalist tragedy *Miss Julie*, which elected for a 1945 setting in the wake of the British Labour party's landslide election victory following the war, was entitled *After Miss Julie* (1996); Polly Teale's recent play for the Shared Experience theatre company which considered the life of novelist Jean Rhys, alluded to her seminal work of appropriation *Wide Sargasso Sea* and its re-vision of *Jane Eyre* in its title, *After Mrs Rochester* (2003). Teale had herself previously adapted *Jane Eyre* for the stage. The term 'after' might seem, then, to endorse postmodernism's beloved idea of belatedness. 'After' can be a purely temporal epithet; a work that is later in date chronologically necessarily comes after. But 'after' can also mean allusive to or referential as in the above examples from Gross, Marber, and Teale: in imitation of, in the style of, alluding to. Yet could we not also riff on the word further and suggest that to go 'after' something would be to pursue it or chase it? The drive of many of the appropriations studied here to go 'after' certain canonical works and question their basis in patriarchal or imperial cultural contexts is an important act of questioning as well as imitative in its modes and gestures. The theoretical and ideological forces that can be seen at play in many of our focus texts cannot be underestimated in this respect. Postcolonialism, feminism and gender studies, queer theory and postmodernism have all wrought important influences on these texts, often equal to and sometimes in excess of the canonical texts or events to which they explicitly refer.

All creative work in the late twentieth and early twenty-first centuries would, however, in postmodernist accounts necessarily come 'afterwards' because nothing new, nothing original, be it in the domain of art, music, film, or literature, is possible any more. We come too late to do anything unique. 'After' in this context becomes a signifier of reduced or debased value: 'that is the best book on the subject after mine'. Those who attack the referential qualities of hip-hop music or digital sampling, bemoan song covers in the popular music charts, or criticize literature's inbuilt intertextualities on the grounds that it stifles individualism, find themselves expounding postmodernism. Those who attacked Graham Swift's novel *Last Orders*, suggesting that it did not deserve literary prizes because it was allusive by nature, because it came 'after Faulkner', and indeed 'after Chaucer' and 'after Powell and Pressburger' as Chapter 2 demonstrates, were voicing comparable views.

'After' need not, though, mean belated in a purely negative sense. Coming 'after' can mean finding new angles and new routes into something, new perspectives on the familiar, and these new angles, routes, and perspectives in turn identify entirely novel possibilities. So we need to find a way of discussing adaptation and appropriation that will register influence but not assume it is a stranglehold, that will see possibility not prescription authored by what comes before, authored by our inheritance, both literary and genetic. The art of adaptation and appropriation has a potent influence and shaping effect in its own right. Recently the very processes and pitfalls of the art of adaptation have served as the raw material for an innovative artistic production: Charlie Kaufman's metafictional, metacinematic screenplay for *Adaptation* (dir. Spike Jonze, 2002) wrestles openly, and with grim irony, with his repeated failure as a screenwriter to adapt on to film in any satisfying way a popular work of non-fiction, Susan Orleans's *The Orchid Thief*. Kaufman's plot actively explores the issues of interpolation, alteration, and imagining that form an inevitable part of the process of adaptation. No appropriation can be achieved without impacting upon and altering in some way the text which inspired the adaptation. So influential, indeed, have some appropriations become that in many instances they now define our first experiences or encounters with their precursor work of art. This observation is often made in regard to Jean Rhys's *Wide Sargasso Sea*. Few contemporary readers now approach *Jane Eyre* without an awareness of Rhys's appropriation, or at least of the significance, feminist, postcolonial, and postmodern, of the marginalized character of the 'madwoman in the attic'. As Worton and Still note: 'every literary imitation is a *supplement* which seeks to complete and supplant the original and which functions at times for later readers as the pre-text of the "original"' (1990: 7). 'Supplement' here once again functions in the sub-Derridean sense of a virtual substitute or replacement for the original (Derrida 1976:

141–57). The filtering and mediation of many of the appropriations studied here through other works of adaptation is further proof of this web of intertextuality that once again resists the easy linear structures of straightforward readings of 'influence' that seem to presume a greater value in whatever comes first.

A limited or foreclosed sense of 'the belatedness' of adaptive literature would restrict the capacity of the appropriation to function as a textual force in its own right. A more positive approach is signalled by J. Hillis Miller in his study of multiple versions of the Pygmalion myth. Acknowledging the 'perpetual belatedness' of these versions, Miller nevertheless stresses that they are 'affirmative, productive, inaugural ... they enter the cultural and historical world to change it and keep it going forward' (1990: 243). A potent example of this affirmative movement forward, the dynamic aspect of adaptation argued for throughout this study, is Philip Pullman's recent collection of novels for younger readers, *His Dark Materials*. This trilogy acknowledges its indebtedness to John Milton's seventeenth-century epic poem *Paradise Lost* in its title, which is a direct quotation from the Miltonic narrative. Pullman's secularizing narratives of parallel worlds, *daemons*, and dust also owe much to Milton's eighteenth-century reader and commentator, William Blake, who in his poetry collection *The Marriage of Heaven and Hell* declared that Milton was unknowingly of Satan's party (Squires 2002). Few would wish however to ascribe to either Blake or Pullman the condition of belatedness or a negative label of derivativeness, and yet it is clear that they both come, willingly and deliberately, 'after Milton' in their writings.

Another work that has recently come 'after Milton', but which enacts numerous filtering effects of its own, is Geoffrey Hill's remarkable poetic sequence *Scenes from Comus*. Ostensibly a contemporary rumination on Milton's 1634 occasional masque for the installation of the Earl of Bridgewater as Lord President of the Council of the Marches ('I've not pieced out the story' (2005: 21), Hill stresses), the poem is also a deep reflection on masquing, music, ephemera, and ageing: 'So let there be nothing where it stood, / Ludlow's brief mirage' (62). Dedicated to the composer Hugh Wood on his seventieth birthday, the poem, both in its title and dedication, calls into focus Wood's own allusive symphony, *Scenes from Comus*, first performed in 1965, and also based on Milton's masque. Once again the process of adaptation proves multi-layered and endlessly plural in its gestures and effects, a version, dare we suggest, of Louis MacNeice's sense in his poem 'Snow' of the 'drunkenness of things being various' (1966: 30).

We need then to restore to the subgenres or practices of adaptation and appropriation a genuinely celebratory comprehension of their capacity for creativity, and for comment and critique. The pleasurable aspect of recognizing the intertextual relationships between appropriations and their sources has been identified throughout this study. The discipline of English Literature, while it cannot easily be reduced to a detective-like mode of cracking ciphers and recognizing allusions, nevertheless thrives on the practices of reading 'alongside', of comparison and contrast, and of identifying intertexts and analogues, that are central to the studies undertaken here. Adaptation and appropriation need to be brought out of the shadows in this respect. They are not merely belated practices and processes; they are creative and influential in their own right. And they acknowledge something fundamental about literature: that its impulse is to spark related thoughts, responses, and readings. To return to the quote from Derrida used earlier, 'Perhaps the desire to write is the desire to launch things that come back to you as much as possible in as many forms as possible' (1985: 157–8). Derrida seems here to respond to observations made on the natural world by Darwin a century before: 'But the environment is not monolithic and stable: it is a matrix of possibilities, the outcome of multiple interactions between organisms and within matter' (cited in Beer 1983: 23). Adaptation and appropriation we might add, supplementing, complementing, coming after Derrida and Darwin as it were, are all about multiple interactions and a matrix of possibilities. They are, endlessly and wonderfully, about seeing things come back to us in as many forms as possible.

GLOSSARY

allusion an indirect or passing reference.

analogue an analogous or parallel text.

analogy a correspondence or partial similarity between text, motif, or thing.

archetype an original, a model or prototype. In literature this also refers to a recurrent symbol or motif.

bricolage in a literary context, a collage or collection of different allusions, quotations, and references in the context of a new creative work. Often associated with the work of structural anthropologists such as Claude Lévi-Strauss who studied the transformations of myth (2001 [1978]) and with postmodernism (Barry 1995: 83).The term derives from the French for Do-it-Yourself (DIY).

citation a passage cited or quoted, with the embedded legal sense of reference to works of authority.

defamiliarization A term frequently deployed in Structuralist and Russian Formalist theory to describe the process of rendering something unfamiliar, especially in literature. Often used to describe the theatrical operations of Bertolt Brecht's theory of *verfremdungseffekt* or 'alienation effect' (Counsell 1996: 103). Also links to Sigmund Freud's notion of *unheimlich* or the 'uncanny' or the 'strangely familiar' (1963 [1919]).

hybridity In literature a term deployed to describe a blend, fusion, or compound of influences at the level of both language and form. Often used by critical theorists to refer to intercultural encounters with both a positive and negative slant (see Bhabha 1995: 206–9).

hypertext Gérard Genette's term (1997 [1982]: ix) for the appropriative or adaptive text (see also 'hypotext').

hypotext Genette's term (1997 [1982]: ix) for the source text of any appropriation or rewriting (see also 'hypertext').

imitation a copy; a counterfeit. In music, this term carries the wider sense of the repetition of a phrase in a different pitch. In classical and early modern culture the term was used in a non-pejorative sense, although in postmodern theory it can refer to the purely derivative.

improvisation a composition or performance of music or verse without a script; in appropriation, the term is extended to a work that adapts in a free-form way a precursor or source text. On improvisation in a social and dramatic context, see Greenblatt (1980: 227–8).

intercultural term used to describe texts and performances that seek to deploy strategies, references, and/or techniques from cultures other than that of the originating artist.

interpolation the insertion of words, phrases, characters, or plotlines into a text.

intertextuality Julia Kristeva's term for the permutation of texts by utterances and semiotic signifiers deriving from other texts (1980). Now the term is used more widely to refer to the relationship between literary texts and other texts or cultural references (for a full discussion, see Allen 2000).

metonymy specifically the act of substituting a word denoting an object or action for one denoting a property associated with it, but in its extended use a word or thing used as a substitute or symbol for another. Often opposed to metaphor.

mimesis imitation or representation. The phrase is most commonly associated with Aristotelian theories of imitation and representation. See also René Girard's anthropology-inflected study of mimesis (1988).

montage in film, the process or technique of selecting, editing, or piecing together separate sections of film to form a continuous whole, particularly associated with the work of Sergei Eisenstein in the twentieth century, but in its more extended use a mixture, blend, or medley of various elements; a pastiche. The term is also used to describe the appropriation of existent songs and music in hip-hop and dj-ing by means of 'cut'n'mix' and sampling.

parody a humorous, often exaggerated imitation of author, work, or style (for a full discussion, see Dentith 2000).

pastiche a term deriving from French, which in the musical sphere refers to a medley of references, a composition made up of fragments pieced together (Dentith 2000: 194). Central to accounts of postmodernist theory and practice (see Barry 1995: 83), in the wider domains of art and literature, pastiche has undergone a further shift of reference, being applied most often to those works that carry out an extended imitation of the style of a single artist or writer.

proximation Genette's phrase (1997 [1982]: 304) for an updating or the cultural relocation of a text to bring it into greater proximity to the cultural and temporal context of readers or audiences.

replication the act of copying. In music, this means repeating a phrase one or more octaves above or below the given tone.

revision the action or instance of revising, or revisiting, although the phrase is given a specifically feminist politics by Adrienne Rich as 're-vision' (1992 [1971]).

riff a short or repeated phrase in jazz music, often as a basis for improvisation.

sampling in musicology, the modification or reuse of part of one musical recording in the context of another. Particularly prevalent in the genre of hip-hop.

supplement a thing or part added to a book. In *Of Grammatology* Jacques Derrida debates the notion of supplementarity, since 'supplement' in French can also mean replacement or substitute (1976: 141–57).

synecdoche a figure of speech in which a part is made to represent the whole.

transformation the act or instance of transforming; metamorphosis, change.

travesty a grotesque misrepresentation or imitation of something.

variation the act or instance of varying; a departure from a former or normal condition. In music, this refers to the repetition of a theme in a changed or elaborated form.

version an account of a matter from a particular point of view; a form or variant of a thing as performed or adapted.

BIBLIOGRAPHY

BOOKS AND ARTICLES

Abbott, H. Porter (2002) *The Cambridge Introduction to Narrative*, Cambridge: Cambridge University Press.

Ackroyd, Peter (1990) *Dickens*, London: Sinclair and Stevenson.

Allen, Graham (2000) *Intertextuality*, London: Routledge.

Andreas, James R. (1999) 'Signifyin' on *The Tempest* in Gloria Naylor's *Mama Day*' in Christy Desmet and Robert Sawyer (eds) *Shakespeare and Appropriation*, London: Routledge.

Ashcroft, Bill, Griffiths, Gareth, and Tiffin, Helen (eds) (1995) *The Post-colonial Studies Reader*, London: Routledge.

Atkinson, Kate (1997) *Human Croquet*, London: Black Swan.

—— (2002) *Not the End of the World*, London: Doubleday.

—— (2004) *Case Histories*, London: Doubleday.

Attridge, Derek (ed.) (1990) *The Cambridge Companion to James Joyce*, Cambridge: Cambridge University Press.

—— (1996) 'Oppressive Silence: J. M. Coetzee's *Foe* and the Politics of Canonisation' in Graham Huggan and Stephen Watson (eds), *Critical Perspectives on J. M. Coetzee*, Basingstoke: Macmillan.

Ayckbourn, Alan (1995 [1984]) *A Chorus of Disapproval* in *Plays: One*, London: Faber.

Bakhtin, Mikhail (1984 [1968]) *Rabelais and his World* trans. Hélène Iswolsky, Bloomington: Indiana University Press.

Barnes, Julian (1989) *The History of the World in 10½ Chapters*, London: Picador.

Barry, Peter (1995) *Beginning Theory: An Introduction to Literary and Cultural Theory*, Manchester: Manchester University Press.

Barthes, Roland (1981) 'Theory of the Text' in R. Young (ed.) *Untying the Text: A Post-structuralist Reader*, London: Routledge.

—— (1988) 'The Death of the Author' in David Lodge (ed.) *Modern Criticism and Theory: A Reader*, London: Longman.

—— (1993 [1972]) *Mythologies*, trans. Annette Lavers, London: Vintage.

Bate, Jonathan (1993) *Shakespeare and Ovid*, Oxford: Clarendon.

—— (1997) *The Genius of Shakespeare*, London: Picador.

Baudrillard, Jean (1981) *Simulacra and Simulation*, trans. Sheila Faria-Glaser, Ann Arbor: University of Michigan Press.

Beer, Gillian (1983) *Darwin's Plots: Evolutionary Narrative in Darwin, George Eliot, and Nineteenth-Century Fiction*, London: Ark.

Benjamin, Walter (2003a) 'On the Concept of History' in Michael Jennings *et al.* (eds) *Selected Writings* 4 vols, Cambridge, MA: Harvard University Press.

—— (2003b [1935]) 'The Work of Art in the Age of Its Technological Reproducibility' in Michael Jennings *et al.* (eds) *Selected Writings*, 4 vols, Cambridge, MA: Harvard University Press.

Bennett, Ronan (2004) *Havoc in its Third Year*, London: Bloomsbury.

Bénye, Tamás (2003) 'The Novels of Graham Swift: Family Photos' in Richard J. Lane, Rod Mengham, and Philip Tew (eds) *Contemporary British Fiction*, Oxford: Polity Press.

Bettelheim, Bruno (1975) *The Uses of Enchantment: The Meaning and Importance of Fairy Tales*, London: Thames and Hudson.

Bhabha, Homi K. (1995) 'Cultural Diversity and Cultural Differences' in Bill Ashcroft, Gareth Griffiths, and Helen Tiffin (eds), *The Post-Colonial Studies Reader*, London and New York: Routledge.

Bigsby, Christopher (ed.) (1997) *The Cambridge Companion to Arthur Miller*, Cambridge: Cambridge University Press.

Bloom, Harold (1973) *The Anxiety of Influence: A Theory of Poetry*, Oxford: Oxford University Press.

Boitani, Piero and Mann, Jill (eds) (1986) *The Cambridge Chaucer Companion*, Cambridge: Cambridge University Press.

Bouret, Jean (1968) *Toulouse-Lautrec*, London: Thames and Hudson.

Bowlby, Rachel (1997) *Feminist Destinations and Further Essays on Virginia Woolf*, Edinburgh: Edinburgh University Press.

Brontë, Charlotte (1985 [1847]) *Jane Eyre*, Harmondsworth: Penguin.

Bullough, Geoffrey (1957–1975) *Narrative and Dramatic Sources of Shakespeare*, 8 vols, London: Routledge.

Byatt, A.S. (1991) *Possession: A Romance*, London: Vintage.

Carey, Peter (1985) *Illywhacker*, London: Faber and Faber.

——(1988) *Oscar and Lucinda*, London: Faber.

—— (1997) *Jack Maggs*, London: Faber.

—— (2000) *True History of the Kelly Gang*, London: Faber.

Carr, Helen (1996) *Jean Rhys*, Plymouth: Northcote House.

Carter, Angela (1967) *The Magic Toyshop*, London: Virago

——(ed.) (1990) *The Virago Book of Fairy Tales*, London: Virago.

—— (1992) *Wise Children*, London: Vintage.

—— (1994) *American Ghosts and Old World Wonders*, London: Vintage.

—— (1995 [1979]) *The Bloody Chamber*, London: Vintage.

—— (2001 [1988]) *Fireworks*, London: Virago.

Cartmell, Deborah, and Whelehan, Imelda (eds) (1999) *Adaptations: From Text to Screen, Screen to Text*, London: Routledge.

Chaucer, Geoffrey (1986) *The Canterbury Tales* in *The Complete Works of Geoffrey Chaucer*, F. N. Robinson (ed.), Oxford: Oxford University Press.

Chedgzoy, Kate (1995) *Shakespeare's Queer Children: Sexual Politics and Contemporary Culture*, Manchester: Manchester University Press.

Chevalier, Tracy (1999) *Girl with a Pearl Earring*, London: HarperCollins.

—— (2003) *The Lady and the Unicorn*, London: HarperCollins.

Clark, Sandra (ed.) (1997) *Shakespeare Made Fit: Restoration Adaptations of Shakespeare*, London: Everyman.

Clarke, Marcus (1997 [1885]) *His Natural Life*, Graham Tulloch (ed.), Oxford: Oxford University Press [World's Classics].

Coetzee, J. M. (1987) *Foe*, Harmondsworth: Penguin.

Collins, Wilkie (1999 [1860]) *The Woman in White*, John Sutherland (ed.), Oxford: Oxford University Press [World's Classics].

—— (1999 [1868]) *The Moonstone*, John Sutherland (ed.), Oxford: Oxford University Press [World's Classics].

Connor, Steven (1996) *The English Novel in History 1950–1995*, London: Routledge.

Coombe, Rosemary (1994) 'Author/izing the Celebrity: Publicity Rights, Postmodern Politics, and Unauthorized Genders', in Martha Woodmansee and Peter Jaszi (eds), *The Construction of Authorship: Textual Appropriation in Law and Literature*, Durham, NC: Duke University Press.

Cooper, Pamela (2002) *Graham Swift's 'Last Orders'*, New York and London: Continuum.

Counsell, Colin (1996) *Signs of Performance: An Introduction to Twentieth-Century Theatre*, London: Routledge.

Coupe, Laurence (1997) *Myth*, London: Routledge.

Cox, Philip (2000) *Reading Adaptations: Novels and Verse Narratives on the Stage, 1790–1840*, Manchester: Manchester University Press.

Crimp, Douglas (1982) 'Appropriating Appropriation' in Paula Marincola (ed.) *Image Scavengers: Photographs*, Philadelphia: Institute of Contemporary Art.

Cruz, Amada, Jones, Amelia, and Smith, Elizabeth T. (eds) (1997) *Cindy Sherman: Retrospective*, London: Thames and Hudson.

Cunningham, Michael (1998) *The Hours*, London: Fourth Estate.

Darwin, Charles (1988 [1859]) *The Origin of Species*, Jeff Wallace (ed.), Ware: Wordsworth.

Dasgupta, Rana (2005) *Tokyo Cancelled*, London: Fourth Estate.

de Grazia, Margreta (1994) 'Sanctioning Voice: Quotation Marks, the Abolition of Torture, and the Fifth Amendment', in Martha Woodmansee and Peter Jaszi (eds), *The Construction of Authorship: Textual Appropriation in Law and Literature*, Durham, NC: Duke University Press.

Defoe, Daniel (1985 [1724]), *Roxana*, David Blewitt (ed.), Harmondsworth: Penguin.

—— (1986 [1719]) *Robinson Crusoe*, J. Donald Crowley (ed.), Oxford: Oxford University Press [World's Classics].

DeLillo, Don (1988) *Libra*, Harmondsworth: Penguin.

Dentith, Simon (1995) *Bakhtinian Thought: An Introductory Reader*, London: Routledge.

—— (2000) *Parody*, London: Routledge.

Deppman, Jed, Ferrar, Daniel, and Gordon, Michael (eds) (2004) *Genetic Criticism: Texts and avant-textes*, Philadelphia: University of Pennsylvania Press.

Derrida, Jacques (1976), *Of Grammatology* trans. Gayatri Chakravorty Spivak, Baltimore: Johns Hopkins University Press.

—— (1985) *The Ear of the Other: Otobiography, Transference, Translation*, New York: Schocken Books.

—— (1992) 'Aphorism Countertime', trans. Nicholas Royle, in Derek Attridge (ed.) *Acts of Literature*, London: Routledge.

Desmet, Christy and Sawyer, Robert (eds) (1999) *Shakespeare and Appropriation*, London: Routledge.

Dickens, Charles (1938) *The Letters of Charles Dickens: Volume 3*, Walter Dexter (ed.), London: Nonesuch Press.

—— (1999 [1846]) *Oliver Twist*, Oxford: Oxford University Press [World's Classics].

—— (1994 [1861]) *Great Expectations*, Kate Flint (ed.), Oxford: Oxford University Press [World's Classics].

Dillon, Janette (1993) *Chaucer*, Basingstoke: Macmillan.

DuPlessis, Rachel Blau (1985) *Writing Beyond the Ending: Narrative Strategies of Twentieth-Century Women Writers*, Bloomington: Indiana University Press.

Dyas, Dee (2001) *Pilgrimage in Medieval English Literature, 700–1500*, Cambridge: D.S. Brewer.

Eagleton, Terry (1994 [1981]) *Walter Benjamin, Or Towards a Revolutionary Criticism*, London and New York: Verso.

Eliot, T.S. (1969) *The Complete Poems and Plays*, London: Faber.

—— (1984) 'Tradition and the Individual Talent' in Frank Kermode (ed.) *Selected Prose of T. S. Eliot*, London: Faber.

Ellis, John (1982) 'The Literary Adaptation: an Introduction', *Screen* 23(1), 3–5.

Erickson, Peter (1996) 'Shakespeare's Naylor, Naylor's Shakespeare: Shakespearean allusion as appropriation in Gloria Naylor's quartet', in T. Mishkin (ed.) *Literary Influence and African-American Women Writers*, New York: Garland.

Farquhar, George (1988 [1706]) *The Recruiting Officer*, London: Methuen.

Faulkner, William (1996 [1930]) *As I Lay Dying*, London: Vintage.

Ferris, David S. (ed.) (2004) *The Cambridge Companion to Walter Benjamin*, Cambridge: Cambridge University Press.

Fischlin, Daniel and Fortier, Mark (eds) (2000) *Adaptations of Shakespeare: A critical anthology of plays from the seventeenth century to the present*, London: Routledge.

Forster, E. M. (1985 [1910]) *Howards' End*, Oliver Stallybrass (ed.), Harmondsworth: Penguin.

Foster, Hal (1988) 'Wild Signs: The Breakup of the Sign in 70s' Art', in Andrew Ross (ed.) *Universal Abandon?: The Politics of Post-modernism*, Edinburgh: Edinburgh University Press.

—— (1997) 'Death in America' in Colin MacCabe, with Mark Francis and Peter Wollen (eds) *Who is Andy Warhol?*, London: British Film Institute.

Foucault, Michel (1979) 'What is an Author', *Screen* 20: 13–33.

—— (1984 [1978]) *The History of Sexuality: An Introduction*, trans. Robert Hurley, Harmondsworth: Penguin.

Fowles, John (1985) *A Maggot*, New York: Signet.

—— (1996 [1969]) *The French Lieutenant's Woman*, London: Vintage.

Frayn, Michael (1999) *Headlong*, London: Faber and Faber.

Freud, Sigmund (1963 [1919]) 'The Uncanny' in Philip Rieff (ed.) *Studies in Parapsychology* trans. Alix Strachey, New York: Collier Books.

Frow, John (1988) 'Repetition and Limitation – Computer Software and Copyright Law', *Screen* 29: 4–20.

Gaines, Jane M. (1991) *Contested Culture: The Image, the Voice, and the Law*, Chapel Hill and London: University of North Carolina Press.

Gamble, Sarah (1997) *Angela Carter: Writing from the Front Line*, Edinburgh: Edinburgh University Press.

Garber, Marjorie (1987) *Shakespeare's Ghost Writers: Literature as Uncanny Causality*, London: Methuen.

Gates Jr, Henry Louis (1988) *The Signifying Monkey: A Theory of African-American Literature*, New York and Oxford: Oxford University Press.

Gay, John (1986 [1728]) *The Beggars' Opera*, Harmondsworth: Penguin.

Genette, Gérard (1997 [1982]) *Palimpsests: Literature in the Second Degree* trans. Channa Newman and Claude Doubinsky, Lincoln: University of Nebraska Press.

Gere, Anne Ruggles (1994) 'Common Properties of Pleasure: Texts in Nineteenth-Century Women's Clubs' in Martha Woodmansee and Peter Jaszi (eds), *The Construction of Authorship: Textual Appropriation in Law and Literature*, Durham, NC: Duke University Press.

Gilbert, Sandra M., and Gubar, Susan (2000 [1979]) *The Madwoman in the Attic: The Woman Writer and the Nineteenth-Century Literary Imagination* 2nd edn, New Haven: Yale University Press.

Girard, René (1988) *'To double business bound': Essays on Literature, Mimesis, and Anthropology*, London: Athlone Press.

Gordon, John (1981) *James Joyce's Metamorphoses*, New York: Barnes and Noble.

Gosse, Edmund (1989 [1907]) *Father and Son: A Study of Two Temperaments*, Peter Abbs (ed.), Harmondsworth: Penguin.

Greenblatt, Stephen (1980) *Renaissance Self-Fashioning: From More to Shakespeare*, Chicago: University of Chicago Press.

Greene, Graham (2001 [1951]) *The End of the Affair*, London: Vintage.

Gross, John (ed.) (2002) *After Shakespeare: An Anthology*, Oxford: Oxford University Press.

Hall, Stuart (1972) 'The Social Eye of Picture Post', *Working Papers in Cultural Studies* 2: 71–120.

Hanson, Lawrence and Hanson, Elizabeth (1956) *The Tragic Life of Toulouse-Lautrec*, London: Secker and Warburg.

Hardie, Philip (ed.) (2002) *The Cambridge Companion to Ovid*, Cambridge: Cambridge University Press.

Harrison, Nancy R. (1988) *Jean Rhys and the Novel as Women's Text*, Chapel Hill: University of North Carolina Press.

Hassall, Anthony J. (1997) 'A tale of two countries: *Jack Maggs* and Peter Carey's fiction', *Australian Literary Studies* 18: 128–35.

Hawkes, Terence (1992) *Meaning by Shakespeare*, London: Routledge.

Head, Dominic (1997) *J. M. Coetzee*, Cambridge: Cambridge University Press.

—— (2002) *The Cambridge Companion to Modern British Fiction, 1950–2000*, Cambridge: Cambridge University Press.

Hermans, T. (ed.) (1983) *The Manipulation of Literary Studies in Literary Translation*, London: Croom Helm.

Hesmondhalgh, David (2000) 'International Times: Fusions, Exoticism, and Anti-racism in Electronic Dance Music' in Georgina Born and David Hesmondhalgh (eds) *Western Music and its Others: Difference, Representation, and Appropriation in Music*, Berkeley: University of California Press.

Hill, Geoffrey (2005) *Scenes from Comus*, Harmondsworth: Penguin.

Hoesterey, Ingeborg (2001) *Pastiche: Cultural Memory in Art, Film, and Literature*, Bloomington: Indiana University Press.

Hofman, Michael and Lasdun, James (eds) (1994) *After Ovid: New Metamorphoses*, London: Faber.

Holderness, Graham (ed.) (1988) *The Shakespeare Myth*, Manchester: Manchester University Press.

Huggan, Graham (2002) 'Cultural Memory in Postcolonial Fiction: The Uses and Abuses of Ned Kelly', *Australian Literary Studies* 20: 142–54.

Hughes, Robert (1988) *The Fatal Shore: A History of the Transportation of Convicts to Australia, 1787–1868*, London: Pan.

Hulbert, Ann (1993) 'The Great Ventriloquist: A. S. Byatt's *Possession: A Romance*' in Hosmer Jr, Robert E. (ed.) *Contemporary British Women Writers*, Basingstoke: Macmillan.

Hulme, Peter, and Sherman, William H. (eds) (2000) *'The Tempest' and its Travels*, London: Reaktion.

Hutcheon, Linda (1985) *A Theory of Parody: The Teaching of Twentieth-century Art Forms*, London and New York: Methuen.

—— (1988) *The Poetics of Postmodernism: History, Theory, Fiction*, London: Routledge.

Iser, Wolfgang (2001) 'Interaction between Text and Reader' in Colin Counsell and Laurie Wolf (eds) *Performance Analysis: An Introductory Coursebook*, London: Routledge.

Isler, Alan (1996) *The Prince of West End Avenue*, London: Vintage.

James, Henry (1984 [1880]) *Washington Square*, Harmondsworth: Penguin.

Jones, Charlotte (2001) *Humble Boy*, London: Faber.

Joyce, James (1986 [1922]) *Ulysses*, Harmondsworth: Penguin.

Kaplan, Fred (1988) *Dickens: A Biography*, London: Hodder and Stoughton.

Keen, Suzanne (2003) *Romances of the Archive in Contemporary British Fiction*, Toronto: University of Toronto Press.

Keneally, Thomas (1987) *The Playmaker*, London: Sceptre.

Kennedy, Dennis (1993) *Looking at Shakespeare: A Visual History of Twentieth-Century Performance*, Cambridge: Cambridge University Press.

Knight, Stephen (2003) *Robin Hood: A Mythic Biography*, Ithaca: Cornell University Press.

Krauss, Rosalind (1985) *The Originality of the Avant-Garde and Other Modernist Myths*, Cambridge, MA: MIT Press.

Kristeva, Julia (1980) 'The Bounded Text' in *Desire in Language: A Semiotic Approach to Literature and Art*, trans. Thomas Gora, Alice Jardine, and Leon S. Roudiez, Leon S. Roudiez (ed.), Oxford: Blackwell.

—— (1986) 'Word, Dialogue and Novel', in Toril Moi (ed.) *The Kristeva Reader,* trans. Seán Hand and Léon S. Roudiez, Oxford: Basil Blackwell.

Ledent, Bénédicte (2002) *Caryl Phillips*, Manchester: Manchester University Press.

Lee, Hermione (2003) 'Someone to watch over me', Review of Graham Swift's *The Light of Day*, *The Guardian*, 8 March.

Levine, Jennifer (1990) '*Ulysses*' in Derek Attridge (ed.) *The Cambridge Companion to James Joyce*, Cambridge: Cambridge University Press.

Lévi-Strauss, Claude (2001 [1978]) *Myth and Meaning*, London: Routledge.

McClary, Susan (2001) *Conventional Wisdom: The Content of Musical Form*, Berkeley: University of California Press.

McKendrick, Walter M. (1998) 'The Sensationalism of *The Woman in White*' in Lynn Pykett (ed.) *Wilkie Collins: A Casebook*, Basingstoke: Macmillan.

MacNeice, Louis (1966) *Collected Poems*, London: Faber.

Marber, Patrick (1996) *After Miss Julie*, London: Methuen.

Marsden, Jean I. (ed.) (1991) *The Appropriation of Shakespeare*, Hemel Hempstead: Harvester Wheatsheaf.

Martindale, Charles (ed.) (1988) *Ovid Renewed: Ovidian Influences on Literature and Art from the Middle Ages to the Twentieth Century*, Cambridge: Cambridge University Press.

Mathieson, Barbara (1999) 'The Polluted Quarry: Nature and Body in *A Thousand Acres*' in Marianne Novy (ed.) *Transforming Shakespeare: Contemporary Women's Re-visions in Literature and Performance*, Basingstoke: Macmillan.

Maurel, Sylvie (1998) *Jean Rhys*, Basingstoke: Macmillan.

Merritt, Stephanie (2002) *Gaveston*, London: Faber.

Miles, Geoffrey (ed.) (1999) *Classical Mythology in English Literature: A Critical Anthology*, London: Routledge.

Miller, Arthur (2000 [1953]) *The Crucible*, Harmondsworth: Penguin.

Miller, J. Hillis (1990) *Versions of Pygmalion*, Cambridge, MA: Harvard University Press.

Milner, John (1988) *The Studios of Paris: The Capital of Art in the Late Nineteenth Century*, New Haven: Yale University Press.

Miola, Robert (1992) *Shakespeare and Classical Tragedy: The Influence of Seneca*, Oxford: Clarendon Press.

Morris, Meaghan (1988) 'Tooth and Claw: Tales of Survival and Crocodile Dundee', in Andrew Ross (ed.) *Universal Abandon: The Politics of PostModernism*, Minneapolis: University of Minnesota Press.

Mullan, John (2003a) 'Elements of Fiction: Clichés', *The Guardian*, 12 April, 'Review': 32.

—— (2003b) 'Elements of Fiction: Dialogue', *The Guardian*, 5 April, 'Review': 32.

—— (2003c) 'Elements of Fiction: Interior Monologue', *The Guardian*, 19 April, 'Review': 32

Naylor, Gloria (1992) *Bailey's Cafe*, New York: Vintage.

—— (1993 [1988]) *Mama Day*, New York: Vintage.

ní Fhlathúin, Máire (1999) 'The Location of Childhood: *Great Expectations* in Postcolonial London', *Kunapipi* 21: 86–92.

Novy, Marianne (ed.) (1999) *Transforming Shakespeare: Contemporary Women's Re-Visions in Literature and Performance*, Basingstoke: Macmillan.

Oates, Joyce Carol (1993) *Black Water*, New York: Plumo/Penguin.

—— (2000) *Blonde*, London: Fourth Estate.

Orleans, Susan (2000) *The Orchid Thief*, London: Vintage.

Ovid (1987) *Metamorphoses* trans. A. D. Melville, Oxford: Oxford University Press.

Patterson, Annabel (1987) 'Intention' in Frank Lentricchia and Thomas McLaughlin (eds) *Critical Terms for Literary Study*, Chicago: University of Chicago Press, pp 135–46.

Pavis, Patrice (ed.) (1996) *The Intercultural Performance Reader*, London: Routledge.

Phillips, Caryl (1997) *The Nature of Blood*, London: Faber.

Phillips, Helen (2000) *An Introduction to* The Canterbury Tales*: Reading, Fiction, Context*, Basingstoke: Macmillan.

Poe, Edgar Allen (1998 [1843]) 'The Gold-Bug' in David Van Leer (ed.) *Selected Tales*, Oxford: Oxford University Press [World's Classics].

Poole, Adrian (2004) *Shakespeare and the Victorians*, London: Thomson Learning/Arden Shakespeare.

Porter, Peter (1997) '*Jack Maggs*', *The Guardian*, 18 September.

Powers, Richard (1991) *The Gold Bug Variations*, New York; HarperCollins.

—— (2001 [1985]) *Three Farmers on Their Way to a Dance*, New York: Perennial.

Price, Monroe E. and Pollack, Malla (1994) 'The Author in Copyright: Notes for the Literary Critic', in Martha Woodmansee and Peter Jaszi (eds) *The Construction of Authorship: Textual Appropriation in Law and Literature*, Durham, NC: Duke University Press.

Pullman, Philip (2001) *His Dark Materials*, 3 vols, London: Scholastic.

Pykett, Lyn (1994) *The Sensation Novel from 'The Woman in White' to 'The Moonstone'*, Plymouth: Northcote House.

—— (ed.) (1998) *Wilkie Collins: New Casebook*, Basingstoke: Macmillan.

Rhys, Jean (1985) *Letters, 1931–1966*, Harmondsworth: Penguin.

—— (1987 [1966]) *Wide Sargasso Sea*, Harmondsworth: Penguin.

Rich, Adrienne (1992 [1971]) 'When We Dead Awaken' in Maggie Humm (ed.) *Feminisms: A Reader*, Hemel Hempstead: Harvester Wheatsheaf.

Ricoeur, Paul (1991) 'Appropriation' in Mario Valdés (ed.) *A Ricoeur Reader*, London: Harvester Wheatsheaf.

Roe, Sue (1982), *Estella, Her Expectations*, Hemel Hempstead: Harvester Wheatsheaf.

Roemer, Danielle M. and Bacchilega, Cristina (eds) (2001) *Angela Carter and the Fairytale*, Detroit: Wayne State University Press.

Rothwell, Kenneth (1999) *A History of Shakespeare on Screen*, Cambridge: Cambridge University Press.

Rushdie, Salman (1991) *Imaginary Homelands: Essays and Criticism, 1981–1991*, New York and London: Granta.

Rushdie, Salman (1998 [1988]) *The Satanic Verses*, London: Vintage.

Sage, Lorna (1994) *Angela Carter*, Plymouth: Northcote House.

Said, Edward (1983) 'On Originality' in *The World, The Text, and The Critic*, Cambridge, MA: Harvard University Press.

—— (1993) *Culture and Imperialism*, London: Vintage.

Sale, Roger (1978) *Fairy Tale and After: From Snow White to E. B. White*, Cambridge, MA: Harvard University Press.

Sanders, Julie (2001) *Novel Shakespeares: Twentieth-Century Women Novelists and Appropriation*, Manchester: Manchester University Press.

Sanjek, David (1994) '"Don't have to dj no more": Sampling and the "Autonomous" Career', in Martha Woodmansee and Peter Jaszi (eds) *The Construction of Authorship: Textual Appropriation in Law and Literature*, Durham, NC: Duke University Press.

Savory, Elaine (1998) *Jean Rhys*, Cambridge: Cambridge University Press.

Schumacher, Thomas G. (1995) '"This is a Sampling Sport": Digital

Sampling, Rap Music, and the Law in Cultural Production', *Media, Culture, and Society* 17: 253–73.

Sears, Djanet (2000 [1997]) *Harlem Duet* in Daniel Fischlin and Mark Fortier (eds) *Adaptations of Shakespeare: A critical anthology*, London: Routledge.

Sellars, Susan (2001) *Myth and Fairytale in Contemporary Women's Fiction*, Basingstoke: Palgrave.

Shakespeare, William (1998) *The Complete Works*, gen. eds Stanley Wells and Gary Taylor, Oxford: Oxford University Press.

Showalter, Elaine (1991) *Sister's Choice: Tradition and Change in American Women's Writing*, Oxford: Oxford University Press.

Sim, Stuart (ed.) (2001) *The Routledge Companion to Postmodernism*, London: Routledge.

Smiley, Jane (1992) *A Thousand Acres*, London: Flamingo.

Spivak, Gayatri Chakravorty (1990) 'Reading *The Satanic Verses*', *Third Text* 11: 41–60.

—— (1991) 'Theory in the Margin: Coetzee's *Foe*. Reading Defoe's *Crusoe/Roxana*' in Jonathan Arac and Barbara Johnson (eds) *Consequences of Theory*, Baltimore, MD and London: Johns Hopkins University Press.

—— (1997 [1989]) 'Three Women's Texts and a Critique of Imperialism', in Catherine Belsey and Jane Moore (eds), *The Feminist Reader: Essays in Gender and the Politics of Literary Criticism*, 2nd edn, Basingstoke: Macmillan.

Squires, Claire (2002) *Philip Pullman's 'His Dark Materials' Trilogy*, New York and London: Continuum.

Stoppard, Tom (1990 [1967]) *Rosencrantz and Guildenstern are Dead*, London: Faber.

Swift, Graham (1983) *Waterland*, London: Picador.

—— (1992) *Ever After*, London: Picador.

—— (1996) *Last Orders*, London: Picador.

—— (2003) *The Light of Day*, London: Hamish Hamilton.

Teale, Polly (2003) *After Mrs Rochester*, London: Nick Hern.

Terry, Philip (ed.) (2000) *Ovid Metamorphosed*, London: Chatto and Windus.

Thieme, John (2001) *Postcolonial Con-Texts: Writing Back to the Canon*, New York: Continuum.

Thorpe, Michael (1990) 'The Other Side: *Wide Sargasso Sea* and *Jane Eyre*', *Ariel* 8: 99–110.

Tiffin, Helen (1987) 'Postcolonial Literatures and Counter-Discourse', *Kunapipi*, 9: 17–34.

Todorov, Tzvetan (1990) *Genres of Discourse*, trans. Catherine Porter, Cambridge: Cambridge University Press.

Tournier, Michel (1984 [1967]) *Friday; Or, the Other Island*, Harmondsworth: Penguin.

Tudge, Colin (2002) *In Mendel's Footnotes*, London: Vintage.

Updike, John (2000) *Gertrude and Claudius*, New York: Alfred Knopf.

Virgil (1983) *The Eclogues and The Georgics* trans. Cecil Day-Lewis, Oxford: Oxford University Press.

Wallace, Christopher (1998) *The Pied Piper's Poison*, Woodstock and New York: Overlook Press.

Warner, Marina (1992) *Indigo, or Mapping the Waters*, London: Vintage.

—— (1994) *From the Beast to the Blonde: On Fairy Tales and their Tellers*, London: Chatto and Windus.

Watt, Ian (1957) *The Rise of the Novel: Studies in Defoe, Richardson and Fielding*, Harmondsworth: Peregrine.

Waugh, Patricia (1995) *The Harvest of the Sixties: English Literature and its Background 1960–1990*, Oxford: Oxford University Press.

Webb, Diana (2000) *Pilgrimage in Medieval England*, London and NY: Hambleden and London.

—— (2002) *Medieval European Pilgrimage, c. 700–1500*, London: Palgrave.

Weimann, Robert (1983) 'Appropriation and Modern History in Renaissance Prose Narrative', *New Literary History*, 14: 459–95.

—— (1988) 'Text, Author-Function, and Appropriation in Modern Narrative: Toward a Sociology of Representation', *Critical Inquiry*, 14: 431–47.

Wertenbaker, Timberlake (1991 [1988]) *Our Country's Good*, London: Methuen.

Wheeler, Michael (1994) *English Fiction of the Victorian Period, 1830–1890*, 2nd edn, London: Longmans.

White, Hayden (1973) *Metahistory: The Historical Imagination in Nineteenth-Century Europe*, Baltimore: Johns Hopkins University Press.

—— (1987) *The Content of the Form: Narrative Discourse and Historical Representation*, Baltimore, MD: Johns Hopkins University Press.

Widdowson, Peter (1999) *Literature*, London: Routledge.

Willett, John (ed. and trans.) (1992 [1964]) *Brecht on Theatre: The Development of an Aesthetic*, NY: Hill and Wang.

Wilson, James (2001) *The Dark Clue: A novel of suspense*, London: Faber.

Woodcock, Bruce (2003) *Peter Carey* 2nd edn, Manchester: Manchester University Press.

Woodmansee, Martha and Jaszi, Peter (eds) (1994) *The Construction of Authorship: Textual Appropriation in Law and Literature*, Durham, NC: Duke University Press.

Woolf, Virginia (1981) *The Diary of Virginia Woolf: Volume 2, 1920–24*, ed. Anne Olivier Bell, Harmondsworth: Penguin.

—— (1988 [1923]) 'Mr Bennett and Mrs Brown', in Andrew McNeillie (ed.) *The Essays of Virginia Woolf: Volume 3, 1919–1924*, London: Hogarth Press.

—— (1992 [1925]) *Mrs Dalloway* Claire Tomalin (ed.), Oxford: Oxford University Press [World's Classics].

—— (1998 [1941]) *Between the Acts* Frank Kermode (ed.), Oxford: Oxford University Press [World's Classics].

Worton, Michael and Still, Judith (eds) (1990) *Intertextuality: Theories and practices*, Manchester: Manchester University Press.

Young, Tory (2003) *Michael Cunningham's 'The Hours'*, London and New York: Continuum.

Zabus, Chantal (2002) *Tempests after Shakespeare*, Basingstoke: Palgrave.

Zipes, Jack (1979) *Breaking the Magic Spell: Radical Theories of Folk and Fairy Tales*, London: Heinemann.

—— (1983) *Fairy Tales and the Art of Subversion: The Classical Genre for Children and the Process of Civilization*, London: Heinemann.

—— (1994) *Fairy Tale as Myth: Myth as Fairy Tale*, Lexington: University of Kentucky Press.

FILMS

Almereyda, Michael (dir.) (2000) *Hamlet*.

Blake-Nelson, Tim (dir.) (2001) *'O'*.

Branagh, Kenneth (dir.) (1996) *Hamlet*.

—— (dir.) (1999) *Love's Labour's Lost*.

Camus, Marcel (dir.) (1959) *Black Orpheus (Orfeo Negro)*.

Cocteau, Jean (dir.) (1950) *Orphée*.

—— (dir.) (1945) *La belle et la bête*.

Coppola, Francis Ford (dir.) (1979) *Apocalypse Now*.

Cuarón, Alfonso (dir.) (1998) *Great Expectations*.

Daldry, Stephen (dir.) (2002) *The Hours*.

Diegues, Carlo (dir.) (1999), *Orfeu*.

Greenaway, Peter (dir.) (1991) *Prospero's Books*.

Heckerling, Amy (dir.) (1995) *Clueless*.

Hughes, Ken (dir.) *Joe Macbeth*.

Jarman, Derek (dir.) (1979) *The Tempest*.

Jonze, Spike (dir.) (2002) *Adaptation*.

Kurosawa, Akira (dir.) (1960) *The Bad Sleep Well*.

Luhrmann, Baz (dir.) (1996) *William Shakespeare's 'Romeo + Juliet'*.

—— (dir.) (2001) *Moulin Rouge*.

Madden, John (dir.) (1998) *Shakespeare in Love*.

Olivier, Laurence (dir.) (1948) *Hamlet*.

Powell, Michael adn Pressburger, Emeric (dirs) (1944) *A Canterbury Tale*.

Reilly, William (dir.) (1990) *Men of Respect*.

Robbins, Jerome and Wise, Robert (dirs) (1961) *West Side Story*.

Rozema, Patricia (dir.) (2000) *Mansfield Park*.

Schepisi, Fred (dir.) (2001) *Last Orders*.

Sidney, George (dir.) (1953) *Kiss Me Kate*.

Van Sant, Gus (dir.) (1991) *My Own Private Idaho*.

Welles, Orson (dir.) (1966) *Chimes at Midnight*.

Winterbottom, Michael (dir.) (2001) *The Claim*.

Zeffirelli, Franco (dir.) (1990) *Hamlet*.

MUSIC

L'Arpeggiata and Christina Pluhar, *All'Improvviso: Ciaccone, Bergamasche, & un po' di Follie ...*, Alpha 512.

Ellington, Duke (1999 [1957]) *Such Sweet Thunder*, Sony/Columbia Legacy CD CK 65568

Gould, Glenn (2002) *A State of Wonder: The Complete Goldberg Variations 1955 & 1981*, Sony Classical CD, SM3K 87703 [sleeve notes by Tim Page].

Quadriga Consort (2003) *Ground: Ostinate Variationen*, HARPrecords CD, LA73002 [sleeve notes by Elisabeth Kurz].

Wood, Hugh and BBC Symphony Orchestra (2001) *Symphony and 'Scenes from Comus'*, NMC DO70

INDEX

Related titles from Routledge

Intertextuality
Graham Allen

the NEW CRITICAL IDIOM

'NO TEXT HAS MEANING ALONE'
'ALL TEXTS HAVE MEANING IN RELATION TO OTHER
TEXTS'

Graham Allen's Intertextuality follows all the major moves in the
term's history, and clearly explores how intertextuality is employed in:

- Structuralism
- Post-structuralism
- Deconstruction
- Postcolonialism
- Marxism
- Feminism
- Psychoanalytic theory

With a wealth of illuminating examples from literary and cultural
texts, including special examination of the World Wide Web, this
book will prove invaluable for any student of literature and culture.

Hb: 0-415-17474-0
Pb: 0-415-17475-9

Available at all good bookshops
For ordering and further information please visit:
www.routledge.com

Related titles from Routledge

The Author
Andrew Bennett

the NEW CRITICAL IDIOM

What is an 'author'? In this clearly-structured introduction,
Andrew Bennett discusses one of the most important critical and
theoretical terms in literary studies. Examining the various debates
surrounding the concept of authorship, The Author:

- discusses Roland Barthes's controversial declaration of the
  'death of the author'
- explores concepts of authority, ownership and originality
- traces changing definitions of the author, and the historical
  development of authorship, from Homer to the present
- examines the interaction of debates on intentionality, feminism and historicism with author theory
- considers the significance of collaboration in literature and
  film.

Accessible, yet stimulating, this study offers the ideal introduction to a core notion in critical theory and is essential reading for all
students of literature.

Hb: 0-415-28163-6
Pb: 0-415-28164-4

Available at all good bookshops
For ordering and further information please visit:
www.routledge.com

Related titles from Routledge

The Singularity of Literature
Derek Attridge

'Wonderfully original and challenging'
J. Hillis Miller

Literature and the literary have proved singularly resistant to definition. Derek Attridge argues that such resistance represents not a dead end, but a crucial starting point from which to explore anew the power and practices of Western art.

In this lively, original volume, the author:

- Considers the implications of regarding the literary work as an innovative cultural event
- Provides a rich new vocabulary for discussions of literature, rethinking such terms as invention, singularity, otherness, alterity, performance and form
- Argues the ethical importance of the literary institution to a culture
- Demonstrates how a new understanding of the literary might be put to work in a 'responsible', creative mode of reading

The Singularity of Literature is not only a major contribution to the theory of literature, but also a celebration of the extraordinary pleasure of the literary, for reader, writer, student or critic.

Hb: 0-415-33592-2
Pb: 0-415-33593-0

Available at all good bookshops
For ordering and further information please visit:
www.routledge.com